Table of Contents

Chapter 1: What Is Digital Marketing
- How Did Digital Marketing Begin?
- What Does Digital Marketing Require?
- Who Can Use Digital Marketing?
- How Will I Make Money with Digital Marketing?

Chapter 2: Identifying Income Channels
- Selling Products
- Selling Services
- Affiliate Marketing
- Dropship Marketing
- Choosing the Right Income Channel for You

Chapter 3: Tapping Into a Global Audience
- Why You Need a Clearly Defined Audience
- How to Identify Your Custom Audience
- Discovering Where Your Audience Is

Chapter 4: Interacting with Your Audience
- Hanging Out with Your Audience Online
- Creating a Relationship with Your Audience
- Building Trust and Credibility
- Gaining and Maintaining Positive Momentum

Chapter 5: Digital Marketing Delivery Channels
- Search Engine Optimization (SEO)
- Content Marketing
- Social Media Marketing
- Pay Per Click (PPC)
- Affiliate Marketing
- Native Advertising
- Marketing Automation

- Email Marketing
- Online PR
- Inbound Marketing

Chapter 6: Using Social Media for Marketing
- Why Social Media Marketing Works
- Who Should Be Using Social Media Marketing
- Creating Your Social Media Presence
- Engaging with Your Audience on Social Media
- Combining Social Media Marketing and Other Marketing Strategies

Chapter 7: Creating Organic Content
- What Counts as Organic Content?
- Who Should Be Using Organic Content Creation?
- Creating Social Media Content
- Creating Email Content
- Creating Blog Content
- Creating Video Content
- Combining Organic Content with Other Digital Marketing Strategies

Chapter 8: Targeted Paid Advertisements
- Why Targeted Paid Advertisements Work
- Who Should Use Targeted Paid Advertisements
- Where You Can Use Targeted Paid Advertisements
- Targeted Paid Advertisements That Are Right for Your Business
- Creating Pay Per Click Advertisements
- Creating Native Advertisements
- Combining Targeted Paid Advertisements with Other Digital Marketing Strategies

Chapter 9: Online Marketing Events
- Why Online Marketing Events Work
- Who Should Be Using Online Marketing Events
- Types of Online Marketing Events to Consider
- Hosting a Webinar
- Hosting Product Demonstrations
- Hosting Courses

    Online Marketing with Online PR

    Combining Online Marketing Events with Other Digital Marketing Strategies

Chapter 10: Tips to Help You Succeed

    Keep Your Website Up to Date

    Design and Evolve Your Customer Experience

    Get Your Business on Google

    Master Your Call to Action

    Track Your Performance With Analytics

Chapter 11: Mistakes to Avoid

    Avoid Outdated Marketing Tactics

    Avoid the "Abandoned Profile" Effect

    Avoid Going into Digital Marketing Without a Plan

    Avoid Underestimating the Importance of All Devices

    Avoid Not Diversifying Your Approach for Greater Reach

Chapter 12: The Power of Staying Relevant Through Conflict and Disaster

    Staying Relevant During Regular Times Vs. Peculiar Times

    Leveraging Trends to Stay Relevant

    Avoiding Tacky or Insensitive Campaigns

    Deepening the Sense of Community Within Your Brand

    Engaging In the Way Your Audience Is Engaging

    Keeping Up With the Changing Times

Chapter 13: The Latest Trends in Digital Marketing

    Facebook Is Losing Grounds with the Younger Demographic

    Instagram Is the Most Popular Platform for Younger Kids

    Properly Designed Chatbots Are Excellent for Customer Service

    Messaging Apps Are Excellent Tools for Marketing Through

    Video Content Must Be Used for Your Brand to Stay Relevant

    Context In Your Content Matters As Much As Quality Does

    Email Marketing Campaigns Should Be More Personalized

    Interactive Content Is the Mainstream Marketing Strategy of Choice

Chapter 14: The 2021 Digital Marketing Forecast

- Automation Meets Personalization, and the Balance Matters
- Non-Linear Advertising Captures Attention
- Marketing Automation Is a Powerhouse, and It Must Be Used Correctly
- Voice Search Marketing Is an Essential
- Content Marketing Should Be Content Selling
- Hyper-Targeted Advertising
- Maximizing Your Digital Marketing Budget Will Matter
- Streamlined Marketing Strategies Will Change The Game

Chapter 1: What Is Digital Marketing?

In a very basic sense, digital marketing is any form of marketing that takes place online. If you are marketing on the internet in any way, shape, or form, then you are engaging in digital marketing practice. There are ten recognized forms of digital marketing: search engine optimization (SEO) content marketing, social media marketing, pay per click (PPC) marketing, affiliate marketing, native advertising, marketing automation, email marketing, online PR, and inbound marketing. We are going to touch on each of these marketing styles in this very book!

Before we dig into how you can start digital marketing, we should first cover the basics of understanding where digital marketing comes from, what it takes to get started, and who is most likely to earn the best income from digital marketing. Having a strong understanding of all of this information will help you determine if digital marketing is right for you. It will also start to give you an understanding of what strategies qualify as high quality modern digital marketing, and what strategies are outdated at this point in the digital marketing era.

How Did Digital Marketing Begin?

The first time the phrase "digital marketing" was used was back in 1990 when the first-ever search engine called "Archie" was launched. At the time, developers proposed the possibility for people to one day use the internet for marketing their businesses by having their businesses show up on relevant search lists that would be displayed by Archie.

In 1993, developers created the first ever clickable ad banner, just like the ones you see on the internet today. These ad banners were displayed at the tops of websites just like they are today and were now able to be clicked so that people could instantly arrive on the website of the company selling said products. Just one year later, the first ever internet transaction was made in 1994 using an application that was known as "Newmarket." Two years later, more search engines were introduced, including Yahoo!, LookSmart, HotBot, and Alexa. Later, in 1997, the first-ever social media site known as "SixDegrees.com" was launched. Finally, in 1998, the infamous "Google" was launched.

Following the introduction of all of these websites, platforms like LinkedIn, WordPress, MySpace, Gmail, Facebook, YouTube, Twitter, and MSN were launched. Developers also began identifying new digital marketing strategies like split testing, which is used to help companies launch two separate campaigns at the same time to identify what reaches their target audience most effectively.

What Does Digital Marketing Require?

Digital marketing is one of the easiest marketing strategies to get involved in, primarily because it is inexpensive to start and because the information is available for virtually anyone to access. In other words, as long as you can read and apply the information that you are learning about, you can take advantage of digital marketing to earn an income in your business, or to develop a business to earn an income from in the first place.

Unlike traditional advertising, which could cost upwards of $250+ to start, digital marketing can cost as little as $100 or less to get started, and it can earn you a decent income in relatively minimal timing. That is why there are so many success stories out there of people replacing their traditional income and even replacing their traditional income ten times over in a matter of a few months to a year. The big key is using your startup budget effectively and set up the right tools so that you have something in place to make money from in the first place. That is exactly what you are going to discover right here in this very book, meaning that as long as you apply these techniques, have some time on your hand, and have a few bucks to start up, you have everything that you need!

Who Can Use Digital Marketing?

Digital marketing can be used by anyone, regardless of where you come from, how much money you have, or whether or not you already have a business in place to sell goods from. As long as you are willing to learn how to make it work and identify a product or service to sell, if you do not already have one, you can take advantage of digital marketing and make it work for you. In this day and age, there are plenty of alternatives to launching your own business or finding your own products or services to sell, which means that digital marketing is more accessible and successful than ever before. As long as you are able to connect with the right companies, you will have everything that you need to make an income with digital marketing.

How Will I Make Money with Digital Marketing?

When it comes to digital marketing, there are two key ways to make money: through selling your own products or services, or through selling someone else's. Below, we will discuss how each of these strategies can earn you an income with digital marketing.

If you want to sell products or services of your own, you are going to need to identify what you want to sell in order to earn an income. If you have a company in place with products or services already, then this is likely not something that you need to consider or worry about. If, however, you are just starting out with building a company that you are going to be selling from, you are going to need to identify something for you to sell. Online, virtually everything sells well as long as you are able to identify and market to your target audience. This means that you can find virtually any product, whether it is physical or digital, or any service and create a market for it. If you want to have greater ease with selling your products or services, it is ideal to do some basic research to identify what types of products or services are selling best at that time. Following the trends and offering trending products or services is the best opportunity that you have to easily access a buying market and offload your products or services quickly so that you can earn an income.

When it comes to offering your own products or services, you should know that this is a less passive form of digital marketing income than the alternative. This way, you may need to be involved in directly shipping or supplying the products, or fulfilling the service requests, which can take quite a bit of time. Of course, if you have the income, you can always hire someone else to do this part for you or outsource it to another company, but it will require more effort on your part.

The alternative is to market for someone else. This is often done either through affiliate marketing or dropship marketing, where someone else's company is responsible for receiving and fulfilling orders, and all you have to do is market for them so that they receive these orders. This way, you are paid a commission per each customer that you send through to make a purchase, which earns you an income. For people who want to create a truly passive income and who do not have the time, funds, or desire to hire anyone else to fulfill these services for them, affiliate marketing or dropship marketing is often the best way to go.

Both of these marketing styles will be done with the same digital marketing tools, and both have the capacity to earn you an income. You will have to determine which one suits your needs best based on how much income you stand to earn, and how much time, effort, and resources it will take on your behalf.

Chapter 2: Identifying Income Channels

If you already have a company in place, then you already know your income channels: they are the products and services that you are already offering your customers. If, however, you do not already have a company in place, you are going to need to identify what your income channels are going to be so that you can discover where you are earning money from with your digital marketing business.

As you know, you can earn money by offering your own products or services, or by marketing for someone else. In this chapter, we are going to discuss four income channels you can explore, as well as what the pros and cons of each channel are so that you can identify exactly the income channel you want to use for your business. This way, you know exactly what you need to be marketing so that you can earn an income with digital marketing.

Selling Products

Designing a digital marketing business selling products tends to be the most labor-intensive digital marketing strategy because, on top of digital marketing efforts, you also need to consider the efforts it will take to manage your inventory. You will need to find a supplier for your products, purchase and receive your products, store your products, and handle and ship your products when they have been purchased. This can take quite a bit of effort on your behalf, so it may be a less passive income source than other digital marketing strategies.

One way that you can make your product-based retail business less labor-intensive is by outsourcing much of the work. For example, if you create a business through Amazon FBA, Amazon will manage everything to do with your inventory, aside from buying and shipping the products to the Amazon warehouse. All you will have to do is identify the products you want to sell, purchase them from a supplier and have them shipped to an Amazon warehouse, and then their employees will take care of the rest. In the meantime, you can use marketing efforts to increase your sales and offload your products quicker. Services like this, however, will cost more to be involved with since you are outsourcing a lot of your businesses work, so unless you want to include the added steps and costs, this may not be the best route.

If you do decide that this is the route for you, however, you can always go ahead and begin identifying products for you to sell online. This way, when you are digital marketing, you know that your focus will be on selling your products, and you can focus all of your efforts on getting people to purchase your businesses products. For some people, this rather traditional approach to retail and advertising is the easiest to comprehend and, therefore, makes the most sense for them to get involved in.

An alternative to this rather traditional form of marketing is to create digital products instead. Digital products include anything from downloadable eBooks to applications or even printable sheets for various purposes ranging from coloring to managing inventory in one's business. You can even make logos, digital graphics, or downloadable patterns, tutorials, or courses for helping people to learn a new skill. There are countless forms of digital products that you can create that can then be sold through digital marketing. If you choose to sell digital products, this becomes a lot easier as you will not have stock to manage in your business. Instead, you simply set up the digital product on a website like Etsy or Shopify and when people purchase if they receive an automatic download file while you receive payment. This can be an excellent way to design a retail shop and earn money from digital marketing, especially because once the products are created, they never need to be remade or reordered again.

Selling Services

Selling services can be another labor-intensive selling style with digital marketing, so understand that if you choose this route, you may not get the time freedom that you desire from your digital marketing business. If you are selling services, you are going to need to prepare to have time to actually fulfill those services after they have been purchased so that people are getting what they paid for. The alternative to fulfilling these services yourself is to hire people who can fulfill them for you, in which case you become somewhat of an agent who recruits people and then finds them work.

Using this income channel with digital marketing, especially if you become an agent, can be a great way to earn an income. There are many different types of services that can be sold online, ranging from consulting services to teaching people a new skill or offering the final product of a valuable skill like writing services or video editing services. As long as you have these skills or abilities yourself, or know of people who do, you can earn a fairly consistent income online through this strategy.

Affiliate Marketing

The most passive form of digital marketing is affiliate marketing. This particular marketing style also has the fewest number of steps to fulfill for you to be able to generate an income from it, as you are simply marketing products for another company.

In order to become an affiliate marketer, you will likely need to have some form of audience and engagement already cultivated online. This way, you can show companies that you are going to be successful in marketing their products because you already have people to market toward, which means you are going to be more likely to receive sales through your digital marketing efforts. For companies who are offering affiliate marketing deals, this is the best opportunity that you have to get in front of them and get a deal with them, allowing you to earn commissions from the sales that you earn for that company.

If you do not already have a healthy audience online, you can still get involved with affiliate marketing, but you will need to choose a different avenue. A common route for people who do not already have a strong online audience is to join an affiliate marketing company that they can earn money from. Affiliate marketing companies, also known as network marketing companies, offer people the opportunity to buy in and then begin marketing for that company. Choosing this method does have its pros and cons, as it can be incredibly lucrative and often comes with a much better compensation plan than standard affiliate marketing agreements. Typically, with a network marketing company, you are paid more if you perform better, so you can earn higher levels of compensation at higher levels within the company. However, it does generally restrict you in terms of what you can market for, as network marketing companies generally don't like it when you market for other companies at the same time.

One of the nicest things about affiliate marketing is that you can get involved with a company and then set up an automated marketing system so that you do not have to do much on a day to day basis to market their products. This way, the automated services run in the background and earn you money without you even having to be directly involved. This specific marketing strategy has earned many people thousands of dollars in passive income every single month, making it a wonderful strategy to use if you are willing to put in the work to set it up and make it successful.

Dropship Marketing

The final income channel you can consider online is dropship marketing. Dropship marketing is similar to affiliate marketing in that you are going to market products for another company, and they are going to oversee everything relating to stocking and fulfilling shipments relating to those products. However, it is completely different in how the business is set up. Unlike affiliate marketing, where you just use and endorse the product, dropshipping generally requires you to set up a business, brand, and a website where you can sell products from. Then, you will upload someone else's products to your website for sale so that people can land on your website and shop the products that you are marketing. When they do, you will get paid a commission, and then the drop shipping company will fulfill the orders of the people who have purchased through your website.

This strategy does require more effort and more funds to get started with than affiliate marketing, but it is also easier to do than selling products or services because you do not have to oversee inventory management and order fulfillment. You will, however, need to get a proper website set up and put effort into establishing and promoting business and brand to people so that they can purchase from you. Once you do establish, however, you can stand to make quite a bit of money as people who are purchasing will be more likely to purchase more products at once, meaning that you can earn a higher commission per sale than you might through affiliate marketing.

Choosing the Right Income Channel for You

Deciding what income channel you want to use is really going to depend on how much effort you want to put into earning sales and making money through digital marketing. Remember that all of the aforementioned income channels will require digital marketing efforts on top of any additional efforts that said the channel would require in order to be fulfilled. For example, selling products will require you to put effort into digital marketing as well as effort into identifying, sourcing, managing, and fulfilling inventory requests.

The best way to decide what strategy is going to be the most effective for you is to determine how much money, time, and effort you want to put into your digital marketing strategy. If you want to be as minimally involved as possible and do not want to invest too much money into your startup, choosing affiliate marketing or network marketing is likely the best income channel for you. If you are interested in putting in more effort, money, and time into your business, you might choose something more intensive, like selling products or services.

After you have identified the best income channel for you, you need to begin educating yourself on how that particular channel works and who you can work with to set it up for you. So, if you choose to be an affiliate marketer, you need to start growing your audience and finding companies that you want to market for so that you have companies that you can earn an income with. Or, if you want to sell products, you need to start researching what products you want to sell and then identifying sources for where you can purchase those products from and places that you can sell those products on. You want to make sure that you identify every person or company that will be involved in making your chosen income channel work so that you have the right people and resources to get started, as well as the right information around what it will take to do so.

Chapter 3: Tapping Into a Global Audience

Once you have identified what income channel you are going to be using, you also want to identify who your audience is going to be and how you are going to tap into them. The nice thing about digital marketing is that you are going to be marketing to an entire global audience, meaning that you can customize your audience in a very specific way, ensuring that you reach exactly the right people for your income channel.

Why You Need a Clearly Defined Audience

Online, billions of people are engaging with various online platforms every single day. Ranging from social media platforms to search engine platforms, there is a massive number of people engaging with the internet on a day to day basis. For this reason, you need to have a clearly defined audience that outlines who you are talking to, and why. If you do not take the time to define your audience online clearly, you are going to have a hard time marketing to anyone because the global market that you are tapping into is simply way too large. Unless you have multiple millions of dollars to invest in marketing, you are not going to be able to tap into a large and undefined audience reasonably.

Clearly defining your audience ensures that you do not waste any of your time, or your budget, on marketing toward people who are not likely to purchase from you. This way, you are spending your time and money on the people who *are* likely to purchase from you, making each click you get on your advertisements more valuable. Think of it this way: if you spend $100 on an advertisement and 1,000 people click it, but only 3 people buy that may not be a valuable advertisement for you since you are not earning much of a return on it. If, however, if you spend $100 on an advertisement and only 500 people click it but 8 people buy from you, you have made a much better earning from that advertisement. This way, you have invested your digital marketing budget in a way that is earning you a better income, making it more worthy of your time and effort. You can make that happen by targeting a very specific audience and spending your entire marketing budget on that audience.

How to Identify Your Custom Audience

Identifying your target audience requires some logic and some research. You will identify your custom audience by first picking the broad audience that you are marketing toward, and then refining that audience so that you have a specific niche that you are catering to.

First and foremost, you want to start identifying your audience by using the logical part of your identification practice. Start by considering what income channel you are using, and who is logically going to be the most likely person to purchase from you. For example, if you chose the income channel of network marketing for a health and wellness company that targets female wellness, logically, your target audience would be women who are interested in personal wellness. This is a broad audience that clearly identifies who you are marketing toward and what your marketing efforts need to look like. This is also a fairly obvious direction to go with your marketing, so there is no need to research whether or not this part of your audience is actually going to purchase from you or not.

The next part of identifying your custom audience is narrowing your audience down to find which niche is going to be most likely to purchase from you. At this point, you want to consider two things: who you are going to be most interested in marketing to, and who is going to be most likely to purchase from you. You need to know who you are going to have the most fun marketing to, because this is going to help you determine who you will have the most knowledge about marketing toward. Generally, the markets you find interesting are also the ones that you understand more intricately, meaning that you will have a clearer understanding of what they need in order to purchase something. In other words, you will know what wording, colors, and placements to use to have success in marketing to them. Ideally, you should identify 3-5 niche markets in your industry that you would have the most fun marketing to. For example, if you were doing the female wellness network marketing company, you might consider targeting working moms, women who live a luxurious lifestyle, women who have a demanding and time consuming career, women who like working out with friends, and women who like attending yoga classes. These types of niches give you the opportunity to clearly identify who you are talking to, and how you can reach them.

Once you have identified 3-5 niche audiences that you could market to, you want to begin researching these audiences so that you can verify that they are going to be profitable audiences. You should pay attention to how large that audience is, how active that audience is, and how likely that audience is to purchase products like the ones that you have available. You also need to determine how easy it would be to market to that audience in terms of how easy it would be to come up with content or sales strategies that would reach and impress that audience enough to encourage them to purchase from you. Ultimately, you want to choose your exact custom audience based on who will be the most likely to purchase from you so that your time, energy, and resources are well invested. This way, not only will you have fun marketing to this audience, but you will also receive great returns on the time that you have invested in marketing to this audience.

Discovering Where Your Audience Is

With your custom target audience fresh in mind, you can begin to discover where your audience is hanging out online so that you can effectively market to them. This means that you need to identify what social media platforms they are using, what e-commerce platforms they spend time on, and where else they are spending time online such as on blogs or forums. Accessing this information is going to ensure that you know exactly where you need to place your digital marketing strategies in order to be seen by the audience that is going to purchase from you.

Because the global audience is so massive and there are countless niches available for people to market in, we cannot reasonably give you every single piece of information regarding the audience that you have chosen for your digital marketing efforts. However, we can give you some basic information about where people are spending most of their time online so that you can get a head start. Then, all you need to do is begin researching your specific audience so that you can really get clear on where they are spending their time.

At this time, consumers are spending their time in three primary areas online: social media and communications platforms, mobile games, and entertainment apps. If you want to get in front of your audience, you are going to need to look in these three areas to see where they are spending most of their time. Pay attention to which specific platforms or apps they are using and downloading so that when you target them, you are placing your ads not only in the right categories but also in the exact places where your audience is likely to see them.

Avoid placing advertisements on apps related to news or website-specific apps, as they are actually decreasing in popularity due to the rising number of "fake news" and click-bait type posts being made by many news and gossip platforms. Placing advertisements on platforms like this will likely result in you not being seen because you are going to be advertising in areas where not as many people are spending their time. Remember, just because 1,000 people see it does not mean that 1,000 people are buying it. You want to be accessing the right audiences where you are going to get more purchases per view, meaning that your budget is being well spent.

Once you know where your audience is spending most of their time, do what you can to test these markets. Do not be afraid to use split testing, or even to spend a small amount of time engaging on your own to see just how engaged these particular audiences are. The more that you can feel confident that you're chosen market is going to be present and visiting your advertisement, the easier it will be to create the right advertisements that are going to earn you sales in your digital marketing business.

Chapter 4: Interacting with Your Audience

Getting into digital marketing is not just about locating your audience but also about interacting with them. Regardless of what income channel you have chosen, there is going to be some level of trust and credibility required in order for people to actually purchase anything that you are marketing. The rapid growth of e-commerce sales and success in recent years has also lead to the rise of many scammers and low-quality companies wasting people's time and money, which means that your target audience already has built-in skepticism. They are not going to buy a product because they saw an advertisement for it, they are going to buy a product because they saw an advertisement from it *through a company or individual whom they trust.*

Fortunately, you do not have to know your audience face-to-face in order to cultivate trust with them, nor do you have to spend many years building up trust with them in order to really generate a large number of sales in your business. All you need to do is prove from Day 1 that you are not selling a scam or low-quality products in exchange for a quick buck so that people trust when they buy from you. This means that if you can establish yourself as being relatable, you can earn your first few sales, which will earn you positive reviews and a positive reputation. From there, you can build on these positive reviews, and the momentum will carry you forward into quick success with your digital marketing business.

In this chapter, we are going to discuss how you can establish this trust and credibility early on so that you can begin building momentum and earning a massive income through digital marketing in minimal timing. Understand that early on, it may take more time, effort, and investment to establish credibility and trust with your audience. However, once you have all you need to do is maintain that credibility and trust, meaning that your own efforts in your marketing strategies will be minimized. This way, you can really begin engaging in digital marketing as a passive income opportunity.

Hanging Out with Your Audience Online

When it comes to establishing credibility and trust with your audience, the first thing you need to do is start hanging out with them online. This is a basic, and perhaps rather an obvious strategy that is going to help you get in front of your audience and begin establishing recognition and a reputation for yourself and your company. Think of it this way: if it was your first day at a new job and you walked into the office and talked to no one, how would people respond? They would probably be curious about you, but concerned about why you were not making an effort to engage with anyone or build any relationships with the people around you. After a few hours, they may grow skeptical about who you are and begin to make up stories in their minds about how you are not trustworthy because you are not making an effort to establish a connection with anyone around you. Others might not even know you were there because you never identified yourself and began connecting with anyone.

If, however, you walked in and immediately introduced yourself and began behaving in a friendly manner, people would recognize that you were nice and would begin to trust in you. Over time, that trust would grow as you continued to establish yourself and prove that you were a trustworthy, hardworking, and relatable employee.

The same goes for establishing your presence online. If you show up and cultivate a presence but never actually use that presence to leverage connections with anyone online, you are going to find yourself being ignored or even judged as an untrustworthy person online. People might begin to believe that you are not safe for them to do business with because they cannot reasonably determine whether or not you are trustworthy or credible, and so they will skip over you and go somewhere else to shop.

You need to get online and actually hang out with your audience in the same areas that they are hanging out. You need to be posting, sharing, and updating your content so that they can see you and get to know you, while also developing a sense of a relationship with you. This way, they know you exist, they can see what you are all about, and they experience positive and memorable first impressions with you and your business. Then, all you have to do is continue to create that relationship so that it grows and your business grows, too. Believe it or not: this does not have to be an incredibly labor-intensive practice, either, as long as it is done right.

Creating a Relationship with Your Audience

The first step to really creating a relationship with your audience is to engage with your audience so that you are not playing the role of the quiet new employee. Engaging with your audience gives them the opportunity to recognize that you even exist, and helps them begin to have a reason to engage back with you. When it comes to marketing, you always have to be the first person to establish a connection with your audience. Otherwise, no one is going to connect with you. Remember, there are thousands of people trying to reach your audience too, no matter how niche you are, so you need to be the one going out of your way to make positive and lasting connections with your own audience.

You can engage with your audience easily by having a social media presence or by establishing yourself on an entertainment platform such as YouTube. This way, your audience has the opportunity not only to discover that you exist but also to see your personality and actually engage with you in a way that contains personalized connection. This is truly one of the key elements in establishing a relationship with your audience so that you can continue to have success in marketing to them.
If you look at any other successful and established a brand, you will discover that they have become masters at creating strong relationships with their audience. They are constantly sharing updates that make their customers feel like they are a part of the "behind the scenes experience," asking questions and creating content that encourages conversation, or engagement, to happen. The more that you can create and post content like this on your platforms, the more success you are going to have in growing your business and building relationships with people online.

The process of creating and sharing content is one of the more time-consuming steps in digital marketing, but it also is a step that is going to offer the highest payoff. Without creating these relationships, it is going to be hard for you to establish yourself and encourage people to purchase from you and your business. Building momentum will be slow, which means that you may never reach the level of success that you desire to reach in your business.

To date, digital marketing has revolved largely around automated marketing. Companies use post schedulers to schedule content for their platforms and use bots to engage with their audience by posting pre-created comments or sending automated messages to new followers or subscribers on their platforms. Automation is still incredibly powerful, and it is necessary if you are going to create a passive income using digital marketing. That being said, going into 2021, you are going to need to adjust how you approach automation to avoid causing your audience to think that you are just another generic, bot-using, spam company selling a low-quality product. Yes, this is a very real reputation that many companies earn by using automation ineffectively, and you are at risk of receiving that reputation if you are not careful in how you automate your business.

Going into 2021, the key to automating your business is to make sure that everything you create is still personable and impressionable. Do not create posts just to create them and schedule them, as this is going to dilute the quality of your posts and, therefore, dilute your reputation in your business. Instead, you need to write content that is meaningful, purposeful, and effective in serving that particular purpose. For example, if you are writing content for the upcoming week, think about what is going to be relevant to your company and what is going to be relevant to your audience. Then, you need to write posts that fill the bridge between what you want to say and what your audience wants to hear.

For example, say you are having a sale on one of your new products in the coming week, and you want to tell your audience about it. For you, you would want to talk about how great the deal is and how much money your audience would be saving because for you, the entire sale is exclusively about earning more money in your business. For your audience, however, the sale is more about getting a great deal on something they want or need in their lives. For that reason, you need to focus on talking about the value of what you are offering and add the sale in as being an excellent way to get their hands on it faster and cheaper. This way, you are marketing for your business in a way that says what your audience actually wants to hear. In other words, you are marketing for your audience, rather than for yourself and your business, which is exactly what it takes to earn more sales online.

In fact, that is exactly what it takes to earn more in your *relationships* online. You need to center your entire approach on serving your audience with what they want and need to hear, but without making it sound like you are just saying these things to make a sale. By now, people have already heard every line out of the book, and for most people, the marketing messages they are reading sound more like a generic pickup line than a strong and authentic marketing message. Understand that people don't mind being marketed to, they just don't like to receive *generic* marketing materials because this is what leads them to believe that your business lacks any personality, authenticity, or uniqueness. Going into 2021, people are more committed than ever to buying products that have a deeper meaning than just serving some form of want or need in their lives. They want to buy products that are serving *them* while also investing in companies that are serving *real* people who own them. They don't want to be investing in some generic company that comes across as being just another soulless corporation. They want to be investing in a person who is passionate about what they are doing and what they are sharing with other people.

Of course, this does not mean that you need to spend every minute of your day engaged deep in passion and obsessing over the products or services that you are offering to other people. However, when you do create and upload content, send out marketing materials, or engage with your audience, it should be clear that you care and that you are a real person. This way, they have someone specifically that they can connect with and establish a relationship with, helping them to have a deeper sense of trust and respect for you and your business.

With this in mind, whenever you automate anything in your business, always write every piece of content with the intention of establishing a real and meaningful connection with your audience, even if it is not *you* responsible for hitting "post" every single day. People can still sense that it is truly you writing your content, or someone who cares, and not just a generic post copied from a marketing blog that the company leverages for money. This way, when people read your content, they connect with it and take time out of their day to engage with it and develop a deeper connection with your company. Then, all you have to do is take a few minutes out of your day or an hour or two out of your week to engage back with everyone who has been engaging with you so that you can establish the two-way connection with your audience. This way, your relationships online will flourish, even if you do not have multiple hours per week to invest in them.

Building Trust and Credibility

As you build your relationships with your audience, you need to use every opportunity that you have to build trust and credibility with your audience. A large part of what is going to establish trust and credibility with your audience is word of mouth, so you are going to need to get people to purchase from or through you and leave positive feedback in order for people to really begin trusting in you. However, you can encourage and grow that trust through how you behave, as well, allowing you to really build on that momentum and grow even further in your business.

The primary keys for establishing trust and credibility between your audience and your brand are the same ones that are going to help you build trust and credibility with other people in your life. These things include honesty, transparency, consistency, devotion, kindness, and considerateness. If you can leverage all of these characteristics in your brand and showcase them in your marketing efforts, you are going to have great success in growing your digital marketing business and earning money online.

Honesty and transparency go hand-in-hand with digital advertising, and they come through how you share with your audience. Businesses that are thought to be honest and transparent are ones who are clear about where their products come from, what values they represent, and what they are offering to their audience. They also tend to showcase the people behind the brand so that their audience can see exactly who is responsible for the company they are shopping with, giving them the opportunity to feel clearer on who they are buying from. You can be honest by letting your customers know why you are selling in the first place, by being honest about where you source your products from, and by being honest about what keeps you committed to offering high-quality service. If you make a mistake or do something wrong in your company in any way, you should also be honest about that as this ensures that your customers know that you are not trying to hide anything. For example, if someone leaves a comment about a negative experience they had on one of your posts, rather than denying responsibility or passing the blame, you should be honest about why that person may have had a negative experience and how you can help them. This way, the customer who had the negative experience feels as though you are being honest and taking responsibility, anyone who reads it feels that you are being honest and taking responsibility, and you are transparent in the experience, too.

Establishing consistency comes from keeping the same image, the same values, and the same approach in your business no matter how long you have been in business for. Consistency shows people that you mean what you say and that you are committed to offering exactly what you said you were going to offer from day one. It also helps establish a clear and consistent reputation for your company, making it easier for people to trust you. This way, people do not begin to question who you are and what you are offering because they see you offering the same things in the same way time and time again. When you are consistent, it also shows that your company is constantly being showcased with the same level of high-quality service and attention to detail that your audience has come to know and expect.

Part of being consistent is being devoted, and showing your devotion to your business, and your audience is also an important part of building trust and credibility with your business in digital marketing. Your audience wants to see that you are devoted to more than just your bottom line by having you show that you care about things like the quality of the products you are marketing and the quality of your customer's experience with your business. If you are not devoted to these things, your customers will believe that the only thing you care about is making a sale, which could translate to you not being overly concerned with the quality of products or services coming along with that sale. In fact, they may even fear that you are willing to cut corners on quality and service in order to earn more money, which is something that no one wants to do business with. Proving your devotion through your content and through how you handle every single customer experience or customer concern establishes credibility and trust within your business, helping you to earn a better relationship with your audience and greater profits.

Although this comes without saying, being kind and considerate in terms of how you market and share with your audience is important. To put it simply: no one wants to do business with a company that is rude, inconsiderate, or impolite. Not only does this mean they are going to have an unpleasant experience with your business, but it could also mean that they are going to experience low-quality products and services. Being kind and considerate in your marketing and in any engagements that you share with your audience will help everyone have a more positive experience. It will also help spread the word about the fact that you are a positive company to do business with, meaning that people will be more likely to do business with you in the first place.

If you are planning on becoming an influencer in 2021, you might be wondering just how you can apply these techniques to your own digital marketing business so that you can earn sales in 2021, too. The key here is simple: you need to make sure that you yourself foster as much of this as you can, and that every business you are affiliated with represents these qualities, too. Showing your audience that every product you recommend comes from a high-quality company and features high-quality manufacturing proves that you are not just going to promote any product that will earn you money. This way, you can establish your own reputation as being the kind of person who promotes products that are actually *good*. As a result, people are going to start trusting in you and seeing you as being a credible resource for helping them to find out what they should buy and who they should buy it from. One of the best benefits of being an influencer this way is that if you only choose to work with highly rated companies, you do not have to work as hard to justify that they are highly rated companies. While you will certainly want to point this out in your marketing content, people will be able to research the companies for themselves and all of the positive reviews they find online will prove that the company is high quality. As a result, they will be far more likely to trust you and invest in the products that you are endorsing.

Gaining and Maintaining Positive Momentum

As you begin to establish momentum by cultivating relationships with your audience and building on your trustworthiness and credibility, you are going to want to keep it going. One of the best tools that you can take advantage of in your digital marketing business is the power of momentum, which is why you need to be willing to stay on top of this momentum to keep your business growing.

Keeping your momentum going is actually easier than establishing it, as all you need to do is continue to create the same level of high-quality content for your audience that you have all along. The key here is remaining consistent and making sure that you are offering the same reputation and image that got you the momentum that you began to build in the first place. If you begin to skimp on your consistency or adapt your image to your growing success in a way that does not seem congruent with the reputation you have already begun to build, you might find yourself losing momentum just as rapidly.

In 2021, the easiest way for you to establish and maintain momentum is to create your business in a way that is sustainable long term. For example, say you are going to establish yourself as an influencer and use digital marketing to earn money by promoting other company's products. In order to successfully do so, you are going to want to start by uploading content and talking about products as often as you plan to in the future. In other words, begin your business by committing in the same way that you anticipate that you will be committing to your business in the future when you achieve the level of success that you desire to achieve. This way, you do not appear to have a sudden change in your approach or reputation the moment you have success in your business, which can lead to suspicious followers and a possible wrench thrown in your reputation, and in your momentum.

Creating your momentum really comes with maintaining your consistency by continually focusing on the same core values, the same purpose behind your work, and the same personality that you launched your business with. In other words, you want to keep doing what you have been doing that launched your success in the first place so that you can continue to be successful.

That being said, every business needs to adapt as they grow, so you are going to want to leave room for change and evolution. As you make a change in your business, make sure that you are doing it in a way that continues to remain consistent with the image and personality that you have built for your business in the first place. This way, people see your changes as being a positive new way for you to serve them, rather than being something that is done with the only purpose of earning more money. Remember, the more that you can make your marketing and business about your client, especially going forward into 2021, the more success you are going to have with your business. This type of approach sets you apart from every other business that is saying "look at me!" because instead, you are saying, "look at you! Here's how I can help you!" This simple switch is mandatory if you are going to stand apart from other businesses in 2021 and really cultivate a deep and meaningful relationship with your audience which, as you know, will ultimately determine the quality of your profits going forward.

Chapter 5: Digital Marketing Delivery Channels

Digital marketing can be done in several ways. However, there are 10 primary ways that people engage in digital marketing in the modern era. Some of these ways have been around for more than two decades now, whereas others are just starting to become more popular in recent years. Regardless of how long they have been around for, virtually every method is receiving a new approach as business owners continue to turn the attention onto their audience instead of themselves. If you want to have success in your business in 2021, the key is to avoid attempting to reinvent the wheel, but instead, spin it at a different angle to achieve your success. In other words, use what is tried and true but build it with the approach of being of service to your audience, rather than being of service to yourself.

In this chapter, we are going to briefly discuss the 10 most popular delivery channels for digital marketing going into 2021, and how you can put a modern spin on these delivery channels. This way, you are using tried and true marketing methods in a way that will serve your business better using the newer, more modern perspective of marketing. If you begin to apply these techniques right away even in 2020, you will find that you are ahead of the curve and that you are able to stand apart from the rest of businesses rapidly, giving you a greater competitive advantage for the 2021 marketing year.

Search Engine Optimization (SEO)

When search engines were invented all the way back in 1990, they needed to have an algorithm that would help them retrieve the proper sites or information for people who were using them. This way, if you searched "cat" you actually received information about cats, and not something random like information about animals in general, or catalytic converters. Without these algorithms, the search results on search engine platforms would likely be low quality, and people would be less likely to use them.

For years now, people have been using SEO to their advantage by seeking to understand how the algorithm for a search engine works and then inputting certain pieces of information into their websites and platforms to improve their search results. This way, they could ensure that they were more likely to show up on the first page, or even as the first search result than anyone else. As a result, they were also more likely to receive the traffic from that particular search, improving their own business results, and helping them generate success through digital marketing.

These days, SEO is certainly not a new term or concept, and it has been described in virtually every digital marketing book out there. However, as algorithms continue to evolve to accommodate growing numbers of searches and search results, the methods required to achieve effective SEO ratings are evolving, too. Going into 2021, you are going to need to improve your organic rankings if you are going to be discovered on search engines like Google, YouTube, Yahoo!, or Bing.

Content Marketing

Content marketing refers to any form of marketing that comes from creating and uploading content to communication or social media platforms. Status updates, blog posts, forum shares, and even link and photo or video sharing on various platforms all count as a variety of content marketing. As you may have gathered from what we talked about in Chapter 4, content marketing is one of the primary methods for establishing a presence and creating a connection and relationship with your audience. Virtually every business that is going to succeed in 2021 is going to need to be using content marketing in one way or another, as we have watched this marketing strategy steadily grow in importance over the past few years.

Creating content to share for your audience can seem intimidating, but as you will learn about in chapter 6, the content that you need to create is actually not too complex, nor time-consuming. You will quickly discover that the key is to produce consistently high-quality content that can be shared on a regular basis, allowing you to get discovered by and connect with your audience. Rather than the "feed the machine" mentality that took shape over the past five or so years where businesses and digital marketers were being instructed to post 3-5 times on each platform every single day, we now realize that this is not necessary. While you do need to have a rather high amount of content being output, there is no need to produce so much content, especially if you do not have that much to say. Instead, producing incredibly high content a few times per week is plenty, which we will discuss more in the next chapter.

Social Media Marketing

Social media marketing and content marketing are closely connected, but understand that social media marketing does have its own purpose aside from content marketing, just like content marketing has its own purpose aside from social media marketing. If you want to establish any level of presence in 2021, you are going to need to be leveraging social media in one way or another. As we have seen in previous years, people turn to social media to learn about the businesses they are considering buying from, and if you do not have a well-established presence there, you are not going to succeed in earning many sales. Social media offers you the benefit of word of mouth, as well as perceived value and credibility, plus it gives you a clear place to establish your presence and leave an impression on a possible customer.

Creating a social media marketing strategy that is passive is not as hard as it may seem, especially because we are moving into an era where the quality of content is far more important than the quantity of the content. This means that rather than trying to upload 3-5 times per day or upload enough content for 3-5 posts per day into an automated poster, you can cut back and produce higher quality content and share it less frequently. The key to really leveraging social media, as you will learn, is to have a strong well-developed profile that immediately showcases who you are and what you have to offer. In the online world, people have a very short attention span, and if you do not capture their interest and set yourself apart from the rest of the world in a matter of seconds, you are unlikely to earn a follower or a sale.

Pay Per Click (PPC)

Pay per click (PPC) advertising is a form of advertising where you produce an advertisement and then pay a larger company like Amazon or Google to display your ad in the ad space that they own around the internet. These types of advertisements, as you may expect from the name, are charged per click, which means that if no one clicks on your advertisement, you are not going to be charged. Similar to native advertising. However, they do come alongside a budget, which means that you determine how much you want to spend, and then launch your ad. The ad will then run until you have received enough clicks to have spent your entire budget.

PPC advertising is an incredibly popular form of advertising that, at one time, was able to exclusively earn thousands of people a high income. In fact, it still has a powerful capacity to help you earn a higher income through digital marketing because the companies that you are advertising through typically have a well-known reputation, which immediately gives you credibility. For example, say you choose to run an Amazon store, and you use Amazon FBA, you could run an advertisement through Amazon, which would then carry the reputation and credibility of Amazon itself. In this way, you do not have to establish credibility for yourself as Amazon has already done that for you, allowing you to put a little less effort into proving yourself. When it comes to marketing, this can have a huge impact and can help you earn an incredible amount of money, especially if you have the right budget and the right demographic being targeted by your advertisements.

Affiliate Marketing

Affiliate marketing was explained in chapter 2 as an income channel, but it also identifies as a specific form of digital marketing. Affiliate marketing is arguably the most "pure" form of digital marketing in that it leverages the power of digital marketing without individuals ever having to touch a product or launch a business. If you become an affiliate marketer, all you are doing is identifying high-quality products and marketing them to your audience. Plenty of affiliate marketers maximize their income by using various other channels of digital marketing ranging from social media marketing and content marketing to PPC and SEO. For many, affiliate marketing is the core structure of their digital advertising business, or it is an added method they use to improve their sales and earn a higher income.

The alternative to becoming an affiliate marketer is recruiting affiliates for your business. If you chose the income channel of selling products or services, recruiting affiliates could help you advertise your products to a broader audience that is already proven, allowing you to save some funds on your advertising fees. For example, if you want to market a new product, putting it in the hands of 3 well-known influencers who are known to produce high sales results can be more effective than spending the equivalent of those products' value on advertising. This is even truer if you are a younger company or one that does not yet have a high level of recognition, as this bypasses the fact that you have yet to build a strong level of trust and credibility within your market.

Native Advertising

Native advertising is similar to PPC, except that instead of being displayed around the internet, it is displayed exclusively on specific platforms. For example, if you run a Facebook page and you launch a Facebook-based advertisement that shows up on people's newsfeeds, you are running a native advertisement on Facebook. Native advertisements are different from PPC advertisements in a sense that they are only displayed within the newsfeed of the social site you chose to advertise on, meaning that it shows up in line with organic posts. For many, this improves results because people see it as being just another post, rather than an actual advertisement displayed in traditional ad space, such as on the side of the screen.

One of the greatest benefits of native advertising is that if you already have an established audience and demographics on your social media sites, you can use these as the audiences that you are going to advertise to. Since they have already begun to pay attention to and engage with your business, these are also people who are far more likely to actually spend money on your business. Advertising to these individuals can pay off big time in the long run, making native advertising one of the most popular paid advertisement strategies of 2021.

Marketing Automation

We have discussed marketing automation a few times in this book, but it is worth pointing out that this strategy is a form of marketing all on its own. People who choose to use marketing automation are engaging in a strategy that enables them to run their businesses in minimal timing, allowing them the maximum amount of time freedom. This is because all of their posts, emails, and advertisements have all been scheduled in advance, meaning they just need to check in from time to time to make sure that everything is running as planned.

Marketing automation is an incredibly powerful tool that can help you really turn your digital marketing business into a passive income stream, so long as you are using it properly. If you want to use this method, you should seek to automate no more than 1-2 weeks in advance, especially going into 2021, as this will allow you to ensure that everything you are posting is relevant and recent. Attempting to automate too far in advance can lead to you talking about things that are completely irrelevant at any period in your business, which can kill your momentum and really make your business suffer?

Another tip with marketing automation is ensuring that you still put the level of consideration and authenticity into each post that you would if you were posting it spontaneously. A big mistake that people have made in the years of 2018-2020 is that they have attempted to create more content in a single day than they can reasonably create, resulting in the content coming out as low quality. For example, in an effort to reduce the amount of time they spend online they may attempt to write all of their posts in just one day, resulting in the quality being lower because at some point they become uninspired, and so they dilute the quality of their content. Furthermore, they have no idea what will be going on in their lives or businesses at that point, making it harder for them to really create posts in advance that still capture attention and share in an authentic manner effectively. Again, choose quality over quantity every single time, and you will already be well ahead of the crowds in 2021.

Email Marketing

Email marketing continues to be a popular marketing resource for people, although it is becoming increasingly apparent that this marketing style is optional. In the past, if you did not have an email list, you were irrelevant and probably not running a successful business. These days, people can successfully run a business without an email list and often do. That being said, an email list is still crucial, as it provides you with a level of security that no other marketing strategy can provide you with.

If you want to be successful with email marketing in 2021, the key is to use this strategy *sparingly*. Many people are receiving 1+ email per day from a single company, causing them to ignore most email marketing campaigns. If you attempt to market through email too consistently, recent studies show that you may actually train your audience to delete your emails rather than look at them because they are tired of having them show up. The simple fact is: virtually no one in your audience wants to hear from you in their email inbox every day. Some don't even want to hear from you more than once a week. Keeping your email newsletters more modest ensures that when your emails show up, people get curious about what you have shared and so they actually open them.

Many businesses aren't even doing that, though.

Many businesses are building email lists and emailing their list just 1-2 times per month, or even less. The reason why they are even bothering to build their lists in the first place is simple: it offers security. In the summer of 2019, we have already seen Facebook and Instagram crash twice, with pictures, status updates, comments, and messenger features not working or only working here and there for many users. While these crashes only lasted one day, they proved to be extremely detrimental to business owners. Think about it: if Facebook or Instagram were to go down for a week, could you make any money? Probably not, because you would not have a way to reach your audience *unless* you had invested time in building an email list. An email list cannot be taken away from you, nor can it "crash." So, if your primary platforms go down, having that email list you built will still give you an opportunity to connect with your audience. Even if you do not plan on emailing your audience frequently, build a list. You will be grateful that you did.

Online PR

PR means that you are gaining coverage on your business from other people. For example, if you launch your business, and a popular blog writes about it, you are gaining PR. Online PR is an important opportunity for you to market your business and establish credibility and authority, while also reaching the eyes of new possible consumers. You want to take advantage of this marketing style so that you can increase your reach and become more recognizable to the people in your audience.

Hiring affiliates to help you market your business is one great way to market using online PR, but there are other strategies, too. One way is to reach out to reporters and journalists and let them know about your business as a way to encourage them to do an interview with your company. However, remember that many other people are doing this too, so you need to do it in the right way if you are going to spark their interest, receive an interview, and maintain the credibility while also boosting the reputation of your company. Attempting to contact them in a pushy or impolite manner can result in you being seen as unprofessional or rude, which can possibly tarnish your business. Remember: they have a large pull in the community!

Other ways that you can engage in online PR include engaging with reviews of your company and engaging with comments made on your website. You can also personally comment or respond back to any comments or emails that come into your business, allowing you to establish yourself and add a personal touch. Any way that you can personally engage with your audience, especially if it is going to be spotlighted in some way for others' to see, is a great opportunity for you to take advantage of online PR.

Inbound Marketing

Inbound marketing is more frequently known as "attraction marketing" in the modern era, and it is an incredibly powerful marketing strategy that you can use to help you get more people coming to you for the products or services that you offer. The biggest benefit of attraction marketing is that you are not pushing customers to buy from you; you are encouraging them to come to the decision of buying from you on their own. In other words, you are attracting them to your business without having to use any form of "used car salesman" tactics.

Inbound marketing is actually a strategy that uses a series of tools to encourage people to do business with you. When you are using this strategy, rather than asking for the sale, you are offering multiple opportunities for the customer to ask you for the sale. For example, using a blog to build interest in your business, creating videos that show off how awesome your products or services are, and using email as a point of contact rather than a constant source of marketing with newsletters are all ways to use inbound marketing. As long as you use tools like this, you will be sure to spark an interest in your audience and encourage them to want to buy from you, rather than pushing for them to buy from you. The difference is that your sales are a lot easier to make, and your reputation improves tenfold because you are seen as someone that people want to buy from, rather than someone that people feel pressured to buy from. In 2021, this particular marketing strategy is expected to grow even more popular than it already has in recent years, so expect to take advantage of it in your own marketing strategy if you actually want to succeed!

Chapter 6: Using Social Media for Marketing

Social media marketing is possibly one of the most well-known forms of digital marketing in recent years. It may also be one of the most powerful strategies to add to your digital marketing efforts, depending on how strong your plan is and how well you execute it. Regardless of what form of company you are running for your digital marketing platform, social media is a tool that you need to be using if you are going to generate any level of success going forward into 2021. In this chapter, we are going to discuss why social media marketing is an essential tool in 2021 and how you can leverage it, as well as how it can be combined with other marketing tools to create a complete digital marketing strategy.

Why Social Media Marketing Works

You may have noticed that we have been stressing one of the most important elements of digital marketing in 2021: *personal connection.* These days, people are tired of service that is automated to the point that it is no longer personal or customizable. They want to receive service that is personal, suited to exactly their needs, and capable of helping them to feel like they are part of something bigger, and something more important. They want to see the "face" behind the business that they are dealing with, and they want to feel like they have some form of connection with the person they are doing business with. That is unless, of course, you have billions of dollars to pour into advertising and state of the art automation services like Amazon, Walmart, or other mega giants do for their online services.

As a beginner, however, you are going to need to create a face for your company that people can identify, get to know, and feel comfortable doing business with. This is where social media comes into play. Social media is a tool that was designed to help people keep in touch. Originally, it was a great opportunity for family members and long lost friends to reconnect and keep up with each other's lives through social sharing. However, it has become an incredibly powerful marketing tool that people can take advantage of, too, especially in that it lets smaller businesses create a name, profile, and personality for themselves online.

When you incorporate social media into your digital marketing strategy, you give yourself the opportunity to create business pages for your company, which allow you to share updates with your audience. In a sense, you give yourself the opportunity to really engage with your audience in a way that feels like you are friends, rather than in a way that feels like you are just another business trying to earn their money. For this reason, social media is one of the most powerful tools for building and maintaining relationships with your followers and customers.

Beyond helping you create a presence that establishes a social connection with your followers, social media has become one of the most popular places for consumers to find new businesses to shop through. These days, platforms like Facebook, Instagram, Twitter, YouTube, Pinterest, and even LinkedIn are all platforms where people are searching for new businesses to shop through. Getting on these platforms and establishing a presence for yourself means that when people begin to look for someone to shop through on these social sharing sites, they come across your profile. If you did not have a profile, they would be less likely to find you.

The reason why social media platforms are becoming a more and more popular platform for people to search for new businesses is that social media sites also come with word of mouth built right in. When a consumer lands on a new profile, they can see just by scrolling whether or not the company is relevant, as well as the quality of services that they offer. Companies that have great engagement with their followers and who seem to have positive relationships with their customers are ones that people will automatically begin to trust, regardless of whether or not they have heard of the company before. Just having a strong social media presence can set the tone for inbound marketing to take place which, as you will learn about, is one great strategy for really leveraging social media marketing.

Who Should Be Using Social Media Marketing

Given the popularity and power of social media marketing, everyone who intends to make any level of money online should be engaging with this marketing strategy. If you want to earn money online, creating a social media presence to make money is a great opportunity. Even if you plan on doing most of your marketing through paid advertisements, establishing a presence and putting up a few organic (non-paid) posts to nurture that presence is a great opportunity to build your business. For most platforms, if you do not have an account, you cannot engage in native marketing, which is one of the most powerful paid marketing strategies that digital marketers can use going into 2021. So, in short, if you are running a business online or plan on making any level of money online, you need to establish some form of presence on social media to help leverage you into higher levels of success with your business.

Creating Your Social Media Presence

The first step in generating a social media marketing strategy is to create your social media presence. For many people, creating a basic presence is all that they will ever need to do, and they use this to leverage their growth elsewhere on the internet. In essence, the social media presence is exclusively designed to help identify new target clients and lead them elsewhere so that they can engage with the business either in person or on their website. For others, their social media presence is their primary source for finding new clients, as well as nurturing those relationships and creating sales. Which method you choose will depend on where your primary sales are being made, and how. If your primary strategy is going to be selling products online on a platform like Amazon, Etsy, Shopify, or Big Cartel, you might favor paid advertisements over organic marketing, and so your presence may be more basic. If, however, your primary strategy is going to be affiliate marketing or running your own business on your own website, you are likely going to need a stronger social media presence to help funnel more people through your sales process.

Creating any level of presence on social media all works in the same way; the only difference is how much you will be posting on your platform. If you only need a basic presence, a few posts per month will be plenty to help you succeed with your business strategy on social media. If you need a bigger presence, you are going to want to post a few times per week, or even a couple times per day, depending on what type of presence you need to establish for success in your digital marketing strategy.

You can start creating your presence by identifying what platforms your audience hangs out on the most and then create a profile on these platforms. When you are creating your profiles, make sure that you are creating them for your business and not for yourself. This means that you need to use your business name, a username that is relevant to your business, and images that are all relevant to your business so that it represents your brand rather than yourself. If you are your brand, pick certain aspects of yourself to highlight on your feed and leave the rest behind. For example, if you are going to become a fashion influencer and leverage digital marketing to earn an income, center your profile around fashion and your passion for design, and leave your love for mechanics out of it. This way, you are creating a profile that is relevant to what your audience wants to be seeing. Later on, when you are more established, it may make sense to begin incorporating smaller amounts of other areas of your life into your presence if you are an influencer, as this gives you a more personal "real" element to you. By sharing small segments of other parts of your life, you show that you are a dynamic person who is interested in many things, not just the one that you market for, which can actually improve your relationship with your followers by increasing your relatability. If you are a specific brand and not an influencer, though, always keep your posting entirely focused on exactly what your brand represents, and nothing more.

These days, there are countless blogs, articles, and books out there telling you about how you can design a branded profile for your social media platforms. That being said, many of them still have a cold, corporate marketing strategy involved that results in you creating a presence that is very isolated from your audience. If you follow many of the strategies that worked in recent years, you may end up building a profile that has an invisible "wall" between you and your audience, making it more challenging for them to connect and resonate with you. You need to make sure that you are cultivating your presence in a way that is open and encourages engagement right from the start so that people feel comfortable connecting with you and doing business with you.

The best way to create this personalized, friendly experience through your platforms is to look at every single element as an opportunity to create a *personal* connection with your audience. Whenever you can, use images that involve faces and language that connects you with your audience. For example, instead of saying, "I am an artist looking to share my art," you could say, "I am an artist looking to share my passions with you." This form of connection-based language helps people instantly feel that the ice has been broken the minute they land on your profile, making it easier for them to engage with the content that you have made available for them to see. When you create this type of personal connection through your language and images, people instantly feel like they are your friend and are more likely to trust in you and all that you have to share with them.

When you first create your presence on social media, in addition to creating a profile, you should also upload at least 3-6 posts right away, or within the first hour or two of creating your profile. This way, whenever someone finds your page, they instantly find some content for them to look at as well, making your profile more worthy of staying on for a while than a bare page. This will also help your early page visitors decide if they want to follow you or not, which will begin to build the momentum of new followers finding and engaging with your page online.

Engaging with Your Audience on Social Media

After you have established your basic presence, you need to start determining how you are going to engage with your audience on social media. This is where you can switch between being someone with a basic presence or someone with a more advanced and engaging presence. The way that you engage with your audience will be the same either way; the only difference will be the frequency of posts you are sharing on that platform. Even if you have a basic presence, you are still going to need to upload at least a couple times per month so that new visitors know that you are still active and not an abandoned profile of a business that may no longer be operating.

When you are engaging with your social media audience, there are three things you need to do: create content, engage with people who engage with your content, and engage with other people's content. All three of these strategies are going to help you grow your presence on social media and build your engagement up more so that you are able to have more loyal followers and more consistent sales through your digital marketing business.

Creating content for your social media will largely be done using content marketing strategies, which we will talk more about in chapter 7. For social media, creating content is going to be the primary foundation of how you connect with other people, so learning how to create proper content for each platform and audience is crucial. Content is what people are going to see and engage with on your profile, and it will give you the opportunity to keep your audience up to date on what you are doing in your business.

Engaging with the people who engage in your posts is important. Especially as a newer business with lower levels of engagement, engaging back with your followers is your opportunity to essentially "reward" their engagement and encourage even more. People like to engage with people who engage back, so the more that you engage with your audience, the more they are going to engage with you, too. They will come to recognize that you are going to engage back and so they will leave their opinions on your posts more regularly, offering you the opportunity to continue engaging back. Not only will this nurture that particular relationship with your business, but it will also show other followers that you engage back and boost your posts through the algorithm of the platform you are sharing on. As your profile grows more popular, it may not be reasonable to try and keep up with every single comment that is made on your posts, so at least taking the time to acknowledge several and comment back to as many as seems reasonable for your help. This way, people see that you are still engaging and that you are still friendly, despite the fact that your profile has grown so massively.

It is also important to go to other people's posts and engage. Especially as a small business, getting your business name out there by engaging with other people's content is going to help you grow faster. You can do this by finding your audience online and then engaging with their content by liking it and, better yet, commenting on it so that they see your profile pop up on their notifications and posts. This way, they may click through and come check out your profile, possibly earning you a new follower for you to engage with on your profile.

Another way that you can engage with other people as you grow your platform is by sharing other people's content. User-generated content, as it is called in digital marketing, is content that other people generate that pertains to your business in one way or another. For example, if someone Tweets about your business or shares a picture of them using your products, this is called "user-generated content." You can then share their images to your own profile and credit them for taking those images, while also sharing a word or two thanking them or acknowledging them for the picture they took. This is a great opportunity for you to acknowledge people who are sharing pictures or updates about your business, while also creating more credibility and awareness for your own profile.

Combining Social Media Marketing and Other Marketing Strategies

Social media marketing can be combined with many other digital marketing strategies. As you have noticed, social media marketing and content marketing tend to go hand-in-hand to help people generate an organic outreach that supports their clients in finding them and engaging with them. Other styles of marketing that combine well with social media marketing include native advertising, affiliate marketing, online PR, automated marketing, and inbound marketing. You can use all of these strategies together with social media marketing to create a well-rounded digital marketing strategy that funnels more sales into your business, allowing you to generate a greater amount of profit from your social media presence.

Which combinations you will use with social media depend on what type of business you are running online? If you are an influencer, for example, you might seek to combine all of these marketing strategies in one way or another to create a complete marketing strategy for your business. If you are a retail store, you might combine social media marketing with native advertising, online PR, and inbound marketing to help you generate more sales in your business. Identify what channels are going to be most effective for you and seek to structure them into a sales funnel, using social media as your primary platform for bringing new followers into your business. These followers can then become leads, and eventually, customers in your business. In other words, social media should always be seen as your first line of contact when reaching new possible clients for your business, no matter what type of digital marketing strategy you plan on using.

Chapter 7: Creating Organic Content

Content marketing has become a more popular topic in recent years, and for good reason. Through content marketing, you have a much greater capacity to create meaningful and memorable relationships with your audience, improving your odds of growing your business through digital marketing. If you are on social media, using a blog, or taking advantage of email marketing, you are going to want to know how to use content marketing effectively to help you succeed. In fact, more recently, content marketing has even been combined with targeted paid advertisements to create an even more powerful impact through these paid pieces of content. Knowing how to create content properly in a way that is going to reach your audience is powerful, and it can be the difference between success and failure in your business.

In this chapter, we are going to explore what organic content is, why it is important, who should be using it, and how you can put it to work in your own business. Understand that virtually every business, no matter what the industry, can benefit from having some knowledge around how content marketing works, so do not overlook this chapter. Furthermore, content marketing has changed drastically in recent months, so understand that anything you may already understand for content marketing may no longer be relevant in this marketing style.

What Counts as Organic Content?

Organic content is any form of content that is shared with your audience without using paid features to improve its odds of being seen. Unpaid social media posts, email newsletters, blogs, and videos all count as organic content. Some people also consider product descriptions and other content uploaded to websites as a form of content creation that falls under the organic content category. Anything that can be consumed either through reading, viewing, or watching, can be considered a form of content, meaning that there are a lot of ways that you can leverage this marketing style to grow your business.

Who Should Be Using Organic Content Creation?

Regardless of what industry you are in, you are going to need to use content in one way or another. Whether you are writing the content for your launch email, updating about a new product in your blog, or sharing something to social media, you are going to be engaging in content marketing. For that reason, everyone needs to be aware of how content marketing works and how it is evolving so that they can take advantage of it and grow their businesses with greater success going into 2021.

Creating Social Media Content

Social media is one of the most well-known places for content marketing to work, as most people are producing content for their social media platforms multiple times per day. Or, if they are combining content marketing with automated marketing, they may be spending an entire day or two creating content and then having that content released on a schedule multiple times per day. Regardless, on social media, virtually everything you post and share to your profile counts as a form of content marketing.

When you are in business, content marketing on social media is important. Due to the volume of marketing that is being done, you need to be mindful of how each piece contributes to your marketing experience, as well as how each piece ties together with other pieces to create an overall image. Unlike emails or blogs, where the content within one email or article stands alone, your social media pages come together to display all of your content in one linear experience, meaning that you need to upload your content strategically. You need to make sure that when people scroll your feed, they have an overall experience where all of the content flows together to create an overall message, rather than all of the content being repetitive experiences of each other. So, where you may be able to send 3 emails in one week about your upcoming launch without having to talk about anything else in between, you will need to be more diversified on your social media posts.

You can diversify your social media posts in many ways, ranging from changing up what exactly you are talking about to how you are delivering that information. For example, say you are going into a launch where you will be releasing a new piece of technology for your customers to purchase. You may do this by uploading a picture of this new device with a caption relating to the device, by uploading a video of someone using your device, and by creating a small write up about why your new device is superior to other devices. In this example, the content has diversified in terms of exactly what is being said or shared, and what medium is being used to share it. Still, the overarching theme remains the conversation around the new piece of technology.

This is exactly how your strategy should be, too. The overarching theme should be relevant to your business and what is presently going on in your business and should continue to remain present in every single post that you make, in a tasteful way. This way, when people land on your page see what you are talking about they can immediately get a feel for what your brand is and what you offer, but they do not feel that your page is spammy or repetitive.

To give you a deeper understanding of how each piece of content can be made in a way that will support its success going into 2021, below we are going to discuss three primary forms of content that are made on social media: written content, graphic content, and video content.

Written Content

One big mistake that people have made in the past when it comes to social media is writing incredibly long posts that do not feature any images or anything else relating to the post. In fact, for the most part, long pieces of written content do not do well on social media in general because it provides way more content than people are typically willing to consume when they are scrolling their newsfeeds.

When you do write content for social media, you want to base its length on two things: who is reading it, and what platform you are using. On a platform like Twitter, for example, the entire point is provided smaller pieces of written content updates on your profile for people to see. For this reason, attempting to put too much-written content is going to get your post ignored, unless you already have a consistent following, in which case you can get away with doing the occasional thread on your feed. On a platform like Facebook, the general consensus is to keep your content smaller. However, you can certainly get away with writing longer texts for your audience, depending on who they are and what type of business you run. On Facebook, texts should range from one sentence to three small paragraphs of content, as anything longer is likely going to lose people's interest. The one exception to this rule is with businesses that are based on your personal story, such as coaching businesses or affiliate marketing businesses where you are sharing your story for marketing. In these circumstances, longer posts with 5-8 paragraphs have been proven to be very effective in helping your content reach and resonate with the right people, improving your odds of being able to market and sell to these individuals. On Facebook specifically, another benefit of writing shorter pieces of content is that the words will be larger than other status updates, which help them stand out from the rest of the posts. Alternatively, you can use a colored background to help your post stand out or stay on-brand, too.

Ideally, most of your content should be shorter if it is exclusively in writing. This ensures that it is short and easy for people to consume, making it more likely that people will actually read it and engage with it. If they agree with what you have shared, they may even share it to their own feeds because it reflects their opinions or feelings, too.

When you are updating social media with something that is exclusively in writing, it is important that you share content that is interesting and complete. Never share an incomplete thought or experience, or something that seems completely irrelevant or pointless, as this is going to dilute the quality of your presence. Remember, you always want your content to make an impact and leave an impression, so use everything from small sentences to longer pieces of content to really get your message across. This way, people will always have respect for you and your business, and they will always see your profile as being worthy of following and paying attention to.

Graphic Content

Graphic content is an incredibly popular form of content marketing on social media, and for most companies, it should be the primary form of marketing that you are using. Graphic content marketing on social media is simple: all you need to do is find a graphic that is relevant to your business and share that graphic with your followers. Many brands will combine graphics content with written content so that they can capture people's attention with the images and then offer their stories or experiences through the written text. In most cases, longer forms of written content will perform much better with a graphic because the graphic encourages people to stop and pay attention to the content in the first place, and it also offers more context to the written word that you are sharing.

When you are sharing graphic content, make sure that everything you share is relevant to your audience. In the modern internet days, it can be easy to get caught up in sharing memes and graphics with your audience to the point where you begin to sway away from what your actual image and purpose is. The simple way to overcome this is to save all non-branded stuff for your personal profile or to ditch it altogether. Even if you think your audience would like a certain image, sharing something that is too off-brand for your business can result in you creating a confusing appearance on social media. Remember, everything needs to remain uniform and consistent if you are going to have success in reaching your audience. Otherwise, even if your audience relates to what you are posting, they may not follow you because they do not know exactly what your purpose is or why they should follow you.

Video Content

Video content works similarly to graphic content, except that instead of images you are going to be posting videos. For many brands, video content works as a great primary form of content on their social media platforms because they build their entire brand around sharing video content for people to watch. For example, if you are an affiliate marketer, you might find yourself using video content to show people the products that you have been using so that they can visually see why those particular products are worth their investment.

With social media, video content can be incredibly powerful in helping people feel more connected with you. You can use video content for everything from showing off new products to live-streaming events that are going on in your business to sharing short video clips of exciting experiences that your company is having. Video content is being leveraged as a way to help bring customers into an exclusive experience with the company that makes it feel like they are right there with the company in whatever the experience may be. For example, if you are having a brand new product launch within your company, you might film the experience of the launch so that people who follow you online can see all of the excitement and build their own excitement, which will likely lead to them purchasing your new product. The more that you can share through video content, the more you are going to help your audience feel close and connected with you and the more they are going to want to purchase from you. Video content is the single form of content that offers your audience the chance to feel face to face with you or your company, so never underestimate the power of a good video.

The key to leveraging video content in 2021 is to make sure that you are sharing content that is high quality, and that breaks the screen barrier with your audience. Even if you have recorded your video privately and not through live stream, can still talk to your audience and ask for their opinion, as they will go ahead and leave their opinions and comments on your video later when it has been uploaded to social media. As much as you can, really play with the fact that video content is meant to make your audience feel like they are right there with you and use that to create a custom, enjoyable experience for your audience.

Creating Email Content

Emails are another form of content marketing that many companies are still using to date. Despite how many people seem to get annoyed by this particular marketing strategy, it continues to be incredibly successful with many companies receiving large volumes of sales through their email campaigns. The key to successfully using email content marketing in 2021 is to create emails that are catchy, interesting, and not overwhelming. In other words, lower volumes of emails with a higher quality of content can go a long way in helping you take advantage of this marketing strategy and reaching your audience through their inboxes.

An alternative to creating email content which has become more popular in 2020, and that will continue to grow in 2021 is using Facebook messenger to create "emails." With Facebook, anyone who messages your business can be messaged in a mass message where you offer updates about your shop and any sales that you may have going on. Using this approach sparingly can be a wonderful opportunity to reach your audience to help let them know what is going on in your business and any other important information that they may need to know about.

When you are creating email content or Facebook messenger content, it is important that you do so effectively. You need to make sure that your emails or messages come across in a way that is polite, informative, and enjoyable to read so that when people open it, they feel compelled to read it all the way through. If your email is too flashy or filled with tacky marketing strategies like clickbait or an excessive amount of sentences that say things like "I'm about to reveal a big secret to you, but first..." you are going to lose people's interest because they will become overwhelmed with or annoyed by the hype in your email. In email marketing, this is the equivalent of walking past a store that has every type of bright flashing light and signs trying to lure people unimaginable, to the point where no one wants to even look at the store, let alone walk in because it is too overwhelming. You also need to make sure, however, that your emails are not too boring. Not offering enough to really draw people through the email can result in them ignoring it because what they are looking at is boring and failing to capture their interest.

The key to email marketing is to keep your email short and value-packed. Your emails should offer three tiers of value, in succeeding order, starting with free content, then full price deals then discounted deals. This way, when people open your email, they see that you are not immediately trying to sell to them in the first sentence of the email. Then, once they have read the free value content, they will see the full priced items as they scroll down to the discounted items, offering them the opportunity to see everything. If you lay your email out in any other way, people may not pay attention because they will assume that your email is just one big advertisement. Although it is, it does not need to look like a flashy, tacky advertisement.

When you are writing the content for your e-mails, keep it friendly and charismatic. Talk to your audience as if you are having a conversation with them, as this will help break the barrier between what you are saying and what they are reading. In a sense, they will feel like they are reading an e-mail from a friend rather than another marketing email in their inbox. This strategy really helps to create that connection experience with your audience, improving the likelihood of them actually reading your emails, and engaging with any of the sales content that you put in it.

In addition to writing content for your emails, make sure that you create strong graphics for your emails, too. These days, basic white-page emails are not going to get nearly as much interaction as ones that are actually designed to match your brand. Using a platform like Mail Chimp or Constant Contact gives you the opportunity to create branded templates that you can then use for your email content marketing. You should make 3-5 branded templates and alternate between them, while also adding additional images into your emails each time you send them out. This way, there is plenty of visual content for people to look at to keep them interested in your emails. If you do not want to have to take so many of your own images for your emails, you can always use a high-quality stock image platform like Unsplash or Pixabay. Remember. However, people do want to have a more personalized experience so you should also include a high-quality image of yourself or someone representing your company in your emails so that your audience gets that face-to-face connection. This will also help them remember who you are since they likely receive many emails from smaller business owners, so this way they remember who they are receiving the email from, why they signed up in the first place, and what drew them to you.

Finally, when you send out emails, you are also going to need a subject line for your email. When it comes to creating email content, your subject line should always be the last thing you write so that it clearly summarizes everything that is going to be inside of the email. This way, you can create a short, quick summary of what is inside in a way that is also inviting and interesting, improving peoples' likelihood of opening the email. For example, if you are announcing your summer sales and you find that your theme has been focused on the wide selection of pineapple decor you have, ranging from pineapple pool floaties to pineapple drink cups, you can use this to create your subject line. In this case, you might make your subject line something like "You + Us = Pineapple" followed by pineapple, sun, and sunglasses emojis. Remember: emojis became popular in email subject lines in late 2018, and they continue to be popular now and going into 2021, so do not be afraid to use a few of them in your subject lines when you are writing emails!

Creating Blog Content

Blog content is similar to emails in that you are going to be creating long handed written content that needs to keep people engaged enough to have them reading everything that you have to share. For the most part, creating blog content has not changed very much in the past few years, as many of the strategies that have already been in action are still incredibly valuable in creating and growing blogs. There are, however, some changes that need to be considered from previous marketing styles that can help you make your blog have even more success online.

To create your blog content, you want to start by picking a topic and then writing about it. Every single blog post should be created with SEO in mind, which means that you need to use specific tools that are going to help search engines recognize your page as being relevant in certain searches, improving your odds of becoming discovered. The four primary things to pay attention to here include keywords, title, paragraph lengths, and images.

When you are writing a blog post, your keyword should be included in your title, and your title should be around 30-50 characters long. Too short of a title can lead to search engines believing that your content is too vague, meaning it may not be as valuable for their audience to read. Instead, they will retrieve an article that seems more relevant, and yours will be left behind.

The keyword that you use in your title needs to be used in your content, too, but it should account for no more than 3% of your entire post. Using it too frequently can result in search engines thinking you are creating spammy content, causing them to lower you in their search results. In addition to using it 3% of the time, you also need to make sure that you are using *exactly* the same keyword that you used in your title. So, if your keyword is "Branding," you need to say the word "branding" in your title and in around 3% of your content that is uploaded into your post. "Brand," "brands," "branded," and any other alternatives to the word "branding" will not qualify toward your keyword percentage, which could result in you not using the keyword enough to be deemed relevant.

Even though blog posts are predominantly written, search engine algorithms know that people do not like to read long pieces of written content without a break in them. When it comes to blogs, a long white page filled with tons of paragraphs is less likely to be looked at than one that has the exact same information but broken up with headlines and photographs. If you want to appeal to the algorithms, you need to refrain from having more than 300-350 words between headlines. This way, you can offer your content in a way that is easier to digest because it draws people's attention through it and offers those breaks in between paragraphs in a complete manner.

Finally, images are a necessary element in your blog posts as they also provide your audience with a visual break in between reading. Ideally, a standard 1,500-word blog post should have 3-4 images in it to help break up the content and offer a more enjoyable viewing experience, in addition to an enjoyable reading experience. When you do upload your graphics, make sure that they are high quality and that they are relevant to your blog so that when people see your page, they see that your content is valuable. You should also make sure that the Meta tags and Meta descriptions of these photographs are relevant by going into the information of the image on your blog and adding a description of what the image is. Since search engines cannot read images, this helps them see that even the graphics are relevant to what people are searching for.

Creating Video Content

Video content is another powerful form of content that can be shared with your audience, but it needs to be done in a tasteful and proper manner. When you are creating videos for your audience, you want to keep your videos 1-10 minutes long, unless you are uploading them on a platform like YouTube where longer videos that are 30-60+ minutes long tend to perform well as well.

When you are creating video content for your audience, make sure that each video has a very specific topic that is relevant to your audience. Then, create a video surrounding that topic that features information around what that topic is, why it is important, and a lesson or two that your audience can learn about the topic itself. This way, when people are watching your video, they have a clear reason behind why they are watching it. The exception to creating videos with lessons is to create videos that are entertaining. However, they should still have a purpose for why people are watching them. This way, people know why they have clicked onto your video, and they feel compelled to continue watching the video until it is done.

In 2021, there is absolutely no room for low-quality videos, so make sure that you are using some basic high-quality filming practices to keep your video worth watching. You can do this by using a camera that shoots in 1080p, or better yet one that shoots in 4k, using natural lighting, and having a visual experience that is enjoyable. This means that you should be well dressed and presentable and that your background should be neat and easy on the eyes. If you are going to be showcasing a product or a certain event, make sure that is clearly visible and that people can easily identify what they are looking at so that they will continue watching. If your video is too hard to watch because it is cluttered or shot in low quality, people are not going to watch it.

Combining Organic Content with Other Digital Marketing Strategies

Organic content marketing can be combined with virtually every other digital marketing strategy. These days, people are using it in everything from native advertising marketing strategies to social media marketing strategies and online PR marketing strategies. Because virtually everything requires some form of content or another, knowing how to create consistently high-quality content that clearly showcases your brand and offers an enjoyable viewing experience is important. Whether you are writing something or sharing a picture or a video, you should always make sure that the message being shared is relevant and that it makes sense to the overall message that your brand stands for. As well, if you will be producing graphics or videos for your content, make sure that the visual experience is relevant, too, by keeping the colors and content of the image or video relevant to your brand. This way, your entire online presence, regardless of where it is being consumed, all fits a similar image.

Chapter 8: Targeted Paid Advertisements

Targeted paid advertisements are well-known in the digital marketing industry, and we have all come across them in our online browsing experiences. In fact, you likely come across them multiple times per day, as they are now placed just about everywhere online! These days, they are placed everywhere from on our social media feeds to our browsing pages, and even on apps and games that we download and play on our phones and computers.

When targeted paid advertisements were originally introduced, the way they were used was significantly different from how we use them today. Back then, companies and website owners would create private deals and then create their own graphics of their advertisements. The company would then pay a website owner a set amount of money for ad space on their website, and the website owner would display the company's ad for a specific period of time. At that time, the deals were virtually always private.

Digital marketers soon caught on to an ideal market niche and began to create advertising agencies. This way, companies and website owners could all go to one agency to be connected with people who were willing to engage in a deal with them. This made it easier for companies to find websites that were relevant to their niche that we ready to create a marketing deal, and it made it easier for website owners to find companies who needed to purchase ad space.

Nowadays, digital marketing is done through mega marketing giants like Amazon, Google, Facebook, Pinterest, and Twitter. All of these platforms are known for offering state of the art technology complete with incredible algorithms that automatically target certain segments of their built-in audience, allowing businesses to market to their ideal audience with ease. This way, anyone who browses online is able to be targeted and have advertisements placed on their feed. As a digital marketer looking to make money through advertisements, this is an incredible advancement that gives you the best opportunity to earn money through your digital marketing efforts.

Why Targeted Paid Advertisements Work

The first step in understanding why targeted paid advertisements work is understanding how they work. These days, every person who browses on the internet has a profile on something or another. These profiles are generally linked to Facebook or Google, or whichever other email service provider the individual may be using during their online browsing experience. When those individual browsers on these platforms, their browsing habits are stored in their "data," which feeds an algorithm that serves a myriad of purposes, including the algorithm that feeds and directs targeted paid advertisements. This means that their specific interests, including products they are curious about and topics they enjoy researching, are fed into the same algorithm that helps targeted paid advertisements, be displayed to the right people.

Once this algorithm is fitted to a person's specific browsing habits, the advertisement company can show these individual advertisements that are more likely to be of interest to them. For example, a person who enjoys cooking and purchasing new small appliances may be identified based on their browsing habits of looking for recipes and researching small appliances. This information would then be uploaded into the algorithm, and they would begin to see targeted advertisements from companies selling small appliances online, especially if they are selling the same type or model that the individual was already looking at.

The system does not rely entirely on the algorithm, though. Businesses are expected to have some basic idea of who they are advertising to so that they can upload these parameters into the technical backend of their targeted paid advertisements so that these algorithms have a general idea of who to advertise to. These two elements combined create the perfect opportunity for your products or services to be displayed to the people who are most likely to purchase your products or services.

The fact that your advertisements are only being seen by the people who are most likely to buy what you have to offer is exactly what leads to this particular marketing strategy being so effective. Now, rather than paying to have a large portion of your audience be individuals who are unlikely to purchase your products, you can feel confident that a large portion of your audience are individuals who are in fact interested in buying what you have to offer. This way, you have a higher conversion ratio, and you are far more likely to earn an income through your targeted paid advertisements.

Who Should Use Targeted Paid Advertisements

Unlike some of the previous marketing strategies we have talked about, targeted paid advertisements are not for everyone. While many businesses will benefit from using targeted paid advertisements, there are people who are going to find that their funds would be better spent elsewhere, at least early on in their marketing experience. The people who are least likely to benefit from targeted paid advertisements are brand new companies who have no credit established in the industry and who are advertising in a way that emphasizes sales rather than recognition.

If you launch a brand new business and from day one your sole focus is on selling products, you are probably going to make sales. However, it will take a long time for you to establish trust and credibility, which means that you may not make as many sales as you could if you chose a different approach. Instead of putting such a massive emphasis on sales, you should be focusing on simply growing brand recognition by using paid targeted advertising that is designed to get more people to land on your profile. Alternatively, you can choose the cheaper route of using organic content marketing to get your business out there and then use paid targeted advertisements after you have established some trust and credibility in your industry.

Another reason why you might not want to begin using targeted paid advertisements right away if you are brand new in business is that you may not know exactly who you are marketing to just yet. Remember, you are tapping into a global audience, which means that you have to know exactly who you are talking to if you are going to be effectively received by an audience unless you have millions of dollars to invest in targeted paid advertising. Investing some time on organic content marketing first is a great opportunity for you to get a clear idea of who is paying attention to your business and who is engaging with you and shopping with you first. This way, when you create your targeted paid advertisements, you know exactly what audience you need to define in your demographic section of the technical backend of your advertisement to have the biggest impact on reaching your audience.

Where You Can Use Targeted Paid Advertisements

There are two types of targeted paid advertisements: pay per click (PPC) advertisements and native advertisements. As you have already learned, PPC advertisements are advertisements that can be displayed anywhere online and that are typically used for one very specific purpose. With PPC advertisements, you are either trying to drive traffic to your website or trying to drive traffic to a specific product or category of products in your business. With native advertisements, you are using a paid feature to ensure that your posts are seen by the right people in your audience, helping to grow more awareness through your social media platforms. Native advertisements can be used to gain more followers, get more traffic to your website, or sell specific products or services through your advertisement.

Targeted Paid Advertisements That Are Right for Your Business

Choosing the right type of paid advertisement for your business is important, as each type of advertisement is going to be displayed in a different location. If you do not get the right location for your advertisement, you are going to struggle to get your advertisement seen in the first place, which means that you could be wasting your entire marketing budget on a misplaced advertisement.

The first and possibly easiest way for a new business to determine what type of advertisement is right for your business is to think about your budget. Generally, PPC advertisements are more expensive and require larger budgets in order to be run anywhere online. Alternatively, social media budgets can be significantly smaller and can still turn a wonderful profit for you as long as you create them properly.

Aside from the budget, there are a few other things that you can consider when it comes to picking the right placement for your advertisement. For example, local businesses generally do better on social media or Google, as they can leverage the structure of each advertising platform to target a local audience. This way, you are not reaching a global audience that you may not yet be ready to serve with your business. Global businesses can generally use any advertising platform as they all also have the capacity to tap into global audiences and be seen by the right people.

You can also consider what specifically you are working on marketing. If you want to increase recognition or engagement, focusing exclusively on social media, advertising is likely going to be your best opportunity to reach the market that you are trying to reach. If, however, you want to advertise a specific product or sale to get more people buying it, Amazon or Google PPC advertisements may be a better option. Social media native advertising can still be effective in helping you sell specific products or market-specific sales, too.

Finally, you need to think about where you want your advertisements to be seen. If you are trying to target an audience on social media, getting on your chosen social media platform and creating a native advertisement is ideal. If, however, you want your advertisements seen on blogs, websites, YouTube channels, and elsewhere on the net beyond social media, you are going to need to design a PPC advertisement with a company like Google or Amazon.

Creating Pay Per Click Advertisements

PPC advertisements are not too challenging to create, although it does take some practice to design an advertisement that is actually going to work. Fortunately, most PPC advertisement backend platforms look fairly similar, and they will walk you through the process of creating an advertisement through their platform

Regardless of what platform you are using for your PPC advertisements, there are five things you need to consider to make sure that you are creating a high-quality advertisement. You need to know: what you are advertising, who you are advertising it to, how much money you have to advertise it with, what you want it to look like, and what you want it to say. These five elements will help you create a well-rounded advertisement that reaches the right audience every single time.

When it comes to what you are advertising and who you are advertising it to, this should be fairly simple. You should have a goal going into every single advertisement, and that goal should help you determine whether you are going to use PPC advertising, native advertising, or both. You want to make sure that you get very clear on what demographic you are advertising to as well, as you need to have a very specific audience that you are targeting your advertisements toward in the backend. You are going to be asked questions about the demographic you are targeting based on what age they are, where they are from, what their interests are, and even how much money they make or what cultural background they have. All of this information helps PPC platforms determine the right audience to show your products to, so you need to have this information so that you can input it into the system. The algorithm will then narrow down the global audience to a specific demographic, and then narrow down your specific demographic into people who are most likely going to buy products from you.

Every single advertising platform requires you to know what your budget is, too. You need to know how much money you are willing to spend over how many days so that the platform knows how much it can spend per click, and when it needs to stop showing your advertisement. If there was no budget and timeline feature, you could risk being charged an enormous amount of money on your advertisements as the platform would not know when to stop showing your advertisement. It is crucial that you pay close attention to the wording around your budget and how long you want to display your ads for, as this part can be confusing. Some platforms will say, "how much do you want to spend *per day?*" and others will say, "how much spending do you want *overall?*" Be very certain that you have read it correctly, as you do not want to put your overall budget as your daily spending limit as this could get expensive, quickly. You also do not want to accidentally put your daily budget as your overall budget as this would result in your advertising not performing well due to not having enough money to really get your advertisement seen by enough people.

When it comes to considering the graphics of your advertisement, you need to think about a graphic that is going to be relevant to what you are advertising, while also being on-brand *and* on-trend. Having all of these elements involved in your graphics will ensure that they are more likely to capture the attention of the person that you are attempting to advertise toward, improving your odds of having them engage with your advertisement. If you are not a graphic designer, it may be worth your while to hire someone who can custom design a graphic that is going to be useful for your advertisement. In general, PPC-style advertisements are usually very simple as they do not want to overwhelm their viewers. Creating a graphic that has too many design elements to it can result in your graphics looking overwhelming, causing people to scroll on by rather than pay attention to it and develop an interest in it.

The alternative to creating a single graphic is creating a video, which can be done for Google-based PPC advertisements. These videos are often shown between other videos that people would be watching online, such as on YouTube. They also occasionally show up on blog posts where the blogger has chosen to add a video-based advertisement to their website. These videos require high-quality video content that is easy to see, clear to understand, and worthy of their time to watch it. Ideally, your video should be filmed with the same level of high-quality attention as commercials on TV would be filmed with, as this is the level of quality that people expect to see when they are watching video advertisements. You also need to make sure that the content of your video is relevant in that it captures the attention of your audience and tells them about what you have to offer them within seconds. If you do not capture their attention within the first 5 seconds of the video, studies have shown that you will likely not capture their attention at all.

After you have created your graphic content, you need to think about the wording related to your PPC advertisement. For some advertisements, the ad will be exclusively wording, so the wording is extremely important. Even for advertisements that feature graphics, however, you need to have catchy phrasing that is going to encourage people to pay attention and actually want to purchase from your business. To create the proper type of written content for your PPC ad, you need to think about where it has been placed. If your ad is being placed somewhere like the top of a Google search, you need to have a clear title and a catchy caption that is going to encourage people to click your link. For example, if you are selling beads online, your ad's title could say "Phoenix Bead Store," and your caption could say, "The largest selection of wholesale beads on the internet!" This type of content clearly displays who you are and what you offer, and gives people the option to click through on your ad and begin to shop for your products.

If you are sharing an advertisement elsewhere, such as blogs, you are also going to need to keep your written content short. On some forms of advertisements, they continue to offer a header and a caption that you can use for your written content. In this case, you would use the same direct, to-the-point, and captivating strategy as we used for "Phoenix Bead Store" above. If, however, you only get one space to write some information in, you want to make sure that you take advantage of it and put the right information in. For advertisements with just one section, you want to be even more direct in your approach. Ideally, you should share no more than 8-12 words about your product so that people do not have to read quite as much in order to get to the point. Something like "Phoenix Beads – Largest Whole Sale Bead Supplier!" is excellent as it captures interest and sells your brand in just a few short words.

Creating Native Advertisements

Native advertisements are actually designed in almost the exact same way that PPC advertisements are made, except that there are some other customizable features that you can take advantage of with native advertisements. If you want to make a native advertisement, you should follow all of the steps outlined in creating PPC advertisements above. However, you can also factor in the following subtle differences that can be taken advantage of to help you make a better advertisement that will likely perform better on social media.

When you are creating a native advertisement, you still need to consider your audience and your specific goal with your advertisement. In these advertisements, the platform you are using will actually let you define a rather specific goal that you want to reach with your advertisement. It is important that you select the right goal for your advertisement as this will go a long way in helping the platform you are using to identify the exact audience for your advertisement to be shown to.

As you create your advertisement, there are generally four styles of advertisements that you can use: you can promote your profile, you can sponsor a post that is already performing well, you can create an advertisement to sell a specific product or service, or you can create a video. All of these advertisement styles are going to be designed exactly according to the PPC standards, except for the following adaptations that you should consider:

Promoting Your Profile

Promoting your profile on social media is like promoting your brand or your website in a PPC advertisement. This is a very basic promotional experience where you are not trying to sell any one specific product, but rather you are looking to boost attention toward your brand and improve brand recognition. On social media, aside from increased followers, one of the biggest benefits of this is faster brand recognition because people are more likely to see and read about your brand several times over in a relatively short period of time. This works much faster than organic content advertising, meaning that it will take less time for you to establish credibility and recognition, as well as grow your following, as long as you are advertising to the right audience.

You can promote your profile on virtually any platform by first ensuring that you are working with a business account. Then, all you have to do is open up the advertisement dashboard of your chosen social media platform and select the goal of "Increasing Brand Awareness" or "Getting New Followers." Both of these goals will help the platform know that you want to get more people landing on your profile. Then, you will follow the same steps of outlining your budget and your audience, choosing your graphic, and creating the written content for your post.

Sponsoring a Post

Sponsoring a post is a style that is unique to native advertising, and it can be an incredibly powerful tool to take advantage of in your business. When you create a post online that performs well, social media platforms allow you to boost that post so that it gets seen by even more people. Boosting posts is a great opportunity to improve brand recognition, while also helping promote whatever the content of your post was. For example, if you were talking about an upcoming launch, and many people liked your post, you could sponsor that post so that even more people would see the content that you were sharing. Plus, because you already have so much engagement on the post, you can identify what demographic (or two demographics) you reached the best with the organic post and target that particular demographic when you sponsor the post. This way, you are getting seen by the right audience, too.

Selling A Product or Service

When it comes to using native advertising for selling a product or a service, the structure of your advertisement will be largely similar to a traditional PPC advertising. You will want to have your product or service highlighted in the graphic of your advertisement, coupled with a few words about what your product or service is and how people can buy or book through you. The two differences of a product or service advertisement being done in this way are that you can add a "buy" or "book" button to most social media advertising platforms. This way, people can click on that button, and it instantly takes them to the page where they can buy or book through you. The second difference is that you can display multiple pictures in a "carousel" advertisement on certain platforms, allowing you to promote and sell multiple products or services in one advertisement.

There is an exception to the written content rule for native advertising when selling products or services, too. When it comes to selling products or services through native advertising, you can use long-form text content depending on who your audience is. In recent years, many people have had a lot of success in writing out a "story" of sorts to help them sell their product or service. This long form text can be used to help create a deeper connection and purpose behind your products, helping people to not only buy into your product or service but to also buy into your brand. This type of promotional post can be extremely beneficial in helping you gain sales and brand recognition and loyalty all at once.

Creating a Video Advertisement

When you are creating a video advertisement for native advertising, the way that you create your video advertisement for PPC advertisements. There truly is no difference between PPC advertising or native advertising with videos, other than the fact that you can add a "buy" or "book" button to your video on the native advertising format.

Combining Targeted Paid Advertisements with Other Digital Marketing Strategies

Targeted paid advertisements can be used in conjunction with virtually every other digital marketing strategy out there. However, you can also use targeted paid advertising as a stand-alone digital marketing strategy that you can take advantage of to sell your products. For example, if you are running an Amazon FBA business as your income channel, you can easily get away with only using Amazon's targeted paid advertising features to promote your products without ever having to create any other digital marketing channel. This way, you keep your income as passive as possible, and you are not required to do anything beyond create, update, manage, and pay for your advertisements, in addition to managing your income channel itself.

Chapter 9: Online Marketing Events

Online marketing events have been rising in popularity since 2005, and have continued to rise through the years. More recently, the way that online marketing events are hosted and how they are leveraged as a marketing tool has changed. These days, it is not enough to simply use your webcam to launch a basic webinar and throw it up on a website and make thousands of dollars through it. Although these methods worked in the past, they are no longer strong enough to really generate enough income for anyone who is using them. If you were to spend your time making things like this, you would find yourself making content that virtually no one was paying attention to because they did not have a strong enough reason to. Elsewhere online, other people would be making higher quality modern content for your audience, and they would likely go to that person instead of you because the content is more enjoyable to consume.

These days, online marketing events are still powerful, but they require a much more personalized approach. You need to be willing to approach them in a way that offers high-quality value, and enough so that it is worthy of people actually investing in it. In other words, you need to refrain from rephrasing something that has already been shared countless times online, you need to deliver your content in a personable and enjoyable manner, and you need to know how to monetize your online marketing event properly. Without these pieces in place, your online marketing event might fall flat and result in you not making a significant impact with your audience.

In this chapter, we are going to discover how you can modernize the outdated webcam webinar so that you can create online events that are going to captivate your audience and have them wanting to do business with you. This way, you can take the strategy that was perfected by previous generations to create a new strategy that is going to be functional in this generation. Going forward in 2021, it is all about quality, personalization, and the fun-factor.

Why Online Marketing Events Work

Online marketing events work for the same reason why any event works: they are fun, and they are easy to build energy and momentum around. Using online marketing events as an opportunity to market to your audience gives you the opportunity to connect with your audience over an enjoyable event while building relationships and encouraging sales to take place in your business. When it comes to online marketing events, you gain all of the same values as you would from an in-person social networking event. You have a mutual interest that has you meeting with other people, you have the opportunity to meet and get to know your audience, and you are given an opportunity to turn the event into a funnel of sorts. Generally, the funnel of an online marketing event looks like this: people have an interest in what you are offering, and they join the event with the intention of learning more. These people may or may not already know about your brand. They sign up to join the event, and then come event day they join in on the event and pay attention to whatever video content is being shared with them. Typically, they also comment and interact through the platform being used, allowing them to have a proper back-and-forth connection with the host. Through this, they get to know the host and whatever the host is talking about, whether it is information, a skill, a product, or anything else that is relevant to the host's business. Once the bulk of the event is done, the host moves into offering a way for them to keep in touch and work together, allowing the attendees to continue to "network" with, or do business with the host. By the end, the people who came and were highly interested in what you have to offer are walking away as new or future clients who are going to bring money into your business.

Who Should Be Using Online Marketing Events

Online marketing events are another form of digital marketing that is not necessarily for everyone. Plenty of product and service-based brands have an easy enough time marketing their products online without ever hosting any form of marketing event, allowing them to thrive without these strategies. That being said, nearly every industry can benefit from using an online marketing event in their business, whether they are selling products or services, or growing their business as an influencer or drop shipper. The key is to choose a creative way to identify how you can connect and share with your audience in a way that helps them feel connected with you so that they can shop through you.

Types of Online Marketing Events to Consider

When it comes to online marketing events, there are four types of events that you can host to help drive more awareness and money to your business. These four event types include webinars, product demonstrations, courses, and online PR. Each of these styles is going to help you generate the level of interest in your business that you need in order to be successful with your sales.

Webinars are an excellent opportunity for any business to communicate with their audience for any number of reasons. Webinars have been hosted to introduce a new business, to introduce a new product, or to talk about why people would be a good fit with a certain business. A popular industry that has used webinars for years is the network marketing industry, where webinars are used to help inform new or prospective marketers on what the business is about and why it would be beneficial for them to join.

Product demonstrations offer businesses the unique opportunity to give their audience a "hands-on" experience with their products through the internet. In the past, salespeople were taught that one of the key ways that sales personnel could encourage people to buy was through getting the product directly into their hands. Test driving cars, trying out a new video game console, or trying on a new outfit were all ways that people could develop a "connection" with the product, making it easier for them to purchase it. Of course, online it is not nearly as easy to create this experience, but it can still be done through product demonstrations. By showing your audience what you are selling and giving them a demonstration of how it works, you can help people determine that your products are worthy of buying and encourage them to make the purchase. This way, you are more likely to make sales online.

Courses are a way that many people have been making money online in recent years. Courses can be used to educate people on certain knowledge or skills which they can then use in their own lives to achieve certain results. Courses can be made on virtually everything from sales strategies and tips to how to do a certain DIY project, depending on what your industry and niche are. There is almost always something that can be taught in any industry, regardless of what you are selling or offering in your business. Creating courses online can be done in two ways: live or evergreen. We will discuss both of these ways in this chapter.

Finally, online PR is a strategy that you can use with online marketing events to help get more eyes on your business. Online PR includes being hosted by popular interviewers on platforms like Facebook or YouTube, or even being hosted by popular interviewers on podcasts. Any opportunity that you have to talk about your business can help you increase awareness around your business while also driving sales into your business. Plus, these PR events help you get in front of a new audience, which will help you get even more eyes on your business.

Hosting a Webinar

If you have decided that hosting a webinar is ideal for your business, you need to begin by choosing what platform you are going to host your webinar on. These days, platforms like Vimeo, Facebook, and Zoom are all great platforms that you can use that allow webinar hosting services to take place. There are four things you need to look for when you are choosing the platform that you are going to host your webinar on: the length of video you are allowed to have, the number of attendees you can have, whether or not people can engage with your videos, and if you can download the video after. You need to have a platform that is going to allow for you to have a video that is long enough to cover your entire webinar, as well as a large enough amount of viewers to make it worth your while. You also need a platform that allows viewers to engage so that you can break the screen barrier and have a positive experience with your viewers. Finally, you need to be able to download the video after so that you can use it in future marketing engagements.

Once you have found the right platform, you need to outline the details of your webinar. First, you need to identify what you want to talk about with your audience. You need to pick a topic that is relevant to your brand, and to your audience, as well as one that is going to provide you with enough content to talk about. Once you have picked your topic, you need to outline about 3-5 main points that you are going to cover in your webinar, depending on how long your webinar is going to be. If you only plan on hosting one for 20-30 minutes, 3 topics should be plenty. If you plan on hosting one for a full hour, you will need about 5 topics to cover so that you have plenty to discuss in that hour.

After you have your topic picked out, you just need to determine what date you are going to host the event on, and at what time. Then, you are going to begin marketing the event. To market your event, you want to get e-mail signups which will allow you to send everyone a reminder through their emails for when the event has started. It will also give you the opportunity to send them the replay, or encourage them to catch a future event if they have missed your webinar. You can encourage people to sign up for the email to get the link to your webinar through social media marketing, targeted paid advertising, and organic content marketing.

In the past, slides were used to offer a slideshow that discussed the topics that the individual was talking about. These days, this is considered impersonal, so avoid doing this on your webinars that you are hosting. Instead, allow the image to be of your face so that people can get a look at you and the screen barrier is broken. This can be more uncomfortable at first, but as you grow used to offering live video-based content, it becomes easier.

Turning your webinars into a monetized feature can be done in two ways. One way is to charge a fee for people to join your webinar, which is only going to work if you plan on offering enough value that they can walk away, having completely learned something from you. The other way is to offer your webinar for free, and then offer something for sale at the end of the webinar. This way, the people who watch it are lead into a sales pitch. You can also combine the free webinar with a paid course and leverage this as a marketing feature by calling your webinar a "freebie" that is added to your paid course, encouraging people to join.

Hosting Product Demonstrations

Product demonstrations, as I mentioned, are the online version of getting your products into the hands of people so that they can feel them and begin to imagine themselves having them in their own day to day life. Using this strategy helps you show people why your products are amazing and why they are worth buying in the first place. When you show people how they work and what they do, you give people the opportunity to imagine what it would be like to use that product in their own lives, too. This marketing strategy is so powerful that even children are watching videos of other children playing with toys, only to then go and ask their parents if they, too, can have that particular toy. Many people are using product demonstrations as a way to market their products, and you can, too.

There are a couple of different ways that you can use product demonstrations in your marketing strategy. Some people use them from time to time on their social media platforms, such as doing a spontaneous live stream demonstration on Facebook. Other people have a YouTube channel or social media presence exclusively dedicated to product demonstrations that they leverage to show off the products that they are selling or marketing. These particular strategies work great for companies selling products or services, or influencers who are marketing for another company.

You can create a demonstration video easily by simply getting in front of a camera and showing a product in use. It can be as simple as a quick 30-60 second demonstration, or a longer 5-10 minute demonstration. The key to making it work in 2021 is to use it in a real-world situation and to be genuine about how you are sharing about the product. Avoid using that overly excited, fake-sounding infomercial voice that everyone has grown immune to, as this will cause people to ignore you. Instead, use an excited but realistic voice and be authentic in how you are sharing, as this will help people feel like it really is exciting, and not like you have to fake excitement around the product.

Hosting Courses

Courses can be created in many different ways, including as a text-based course that is hosted on a site and sold as a digital product. For this section, we are talking about a specific style of offering online courses which consist of hosting a live course first and then, if you want to, turning it into an evergreen course, or a course that is offered without a live element.

Hosting courses starts with identifying what you have knowledge about that you could educate someone else on. Then, you want to do all of the same preparation as you would for a webinar by choosing your topic, outlining your teaching points, and planning the date and time. The difference with courses and webinars is that your courses are generally going to happen over 2-3+ sessions, and they do not always offer a sales pitch at the end of the video. That being said, they certainly can offer a sales pitch to encourage people to buy something from you if you desire to leverage the course even further.

You will market your course in the same way that you market a webinar, too, using features like social media marketing, organic content marketing, targeted paid advertisements, and automated marketing features. To get people to sign up, they should be added to an email list where they will then be given information about the course as well as provided with the necessary links to join the live videos.

As you host the course, make an effort to treat each live session, just like a teacher would treat a classroom. Have the goal of introducing information and educating people on this information, and having them leave each "class" feeling as though they have learned something valuable. By the end of the course, they should be able to put everything together as one big lesson that they have learned, with plenty of smaller pieces of information to apply, too.

Once you are done hosting each class, you can download that day's video. Then, in the future, you can put those videos together to make an evergreen course. This simply means that you choose a hosting platform such as Squarespace, Teachable, or Udemy, and you put the content together in the form of a course. You may choose to include workbooks or written content in the course so that there is even more value offered for people who want to join. Then, all you have to do is market that course and people can buy it and take it without you ever having to talk about the content on a video again. Many people have made hundreds of thousands and even millions of dollars this way, making it a wonderful opportunity for you to earn money while actively designing the product that will continue to earn you money.

Online Marketing with Online PR

Online PR with online marketing events is a great combination to market your events with. With online PR, you are not actually hosting the event, but instead, you are being hosted as a guest speaker or guest visitor by someone else who is hosting the event. You can get engaged with online PR by identifying major online interviewers in your industry on platforms like podcasts, YouTube, Facebook, Instagram, and anywhere else where these individuals may be located in your industry. Once you have found those individuals, you can look at their websites and discover what the requirements are to be interviewed by them. Make sure that you always look first and that you approach these individuals in their desired manner, as this shows your own professionalism and makes them more likely to actually want to interview you. If you are rude or if you approach them in any other way, they may ignore you or even respond with something negative, while also possibly disrupting the reputation that you have worked so hard to make. In this case, it is your fault too for not having respected the individual that you were approaching.

Once you have approached an individual, you will work together with them to arrange the online PR event that you will be doing together to help get the word about your business out there. After this, all you have to do is prepare by looking proper if you need to present yourself visually, and by having the right filming or sound equipment available. Then, you simply show up and talk to the individual and complete the interview or the PR event.

Most times, the individual hosting you will want you to do to some level of marketing to your own audience, too. Be prepared to make social media updates, send out emails, and otherwise communicate with your audience to let them know about the interview that you are doing. This not only helps fulfill your own requirements to be a part of the event but also helps get even more eyes on your event. The more that people see it, the more likely even more people will see it, increasing your chances of having success with your online PR marketing event.

Combining Online Marketing Events with Other Digital Marketing Strategies

Online marketing events can easily be combined with social media marketing, organic content marketing, and targeted paid advertising marketing to help you get the word out there about your business. The key to marketing your online event is to choose every avenue that may be possible for you and use it. Most people will start with using social media marketing and content marketing to advertise their events and may use native advertising as a way to get it out there, too. Then, once the event has been done, they will offer a replay of the event and market that, too. At this point, they often use native advertising and PPC advertising as a way to increase the reach even further, making it even easier for you to get in front of a larger audience and grow your business even more.

Chapter 10: Tips to Help You Succeed

Although we can give you a lot of valuable and strategic advice to get you started and thriving in digital marketing, there is one thing that we cannot give you in this book. That is the value of hands-on experience in your marketing strategy. No matter what new strategy or skill you are trying to pick up, there is a certain level of subtle knowledge and intuitive understanding that comes from having actual hands-on experience with what you are doing.

While we cannot give you that specifically, we can give you some information to help you begin to understand these subtle pieces of information, allowing you to step even closer to digital marketing mastery right here, right now. This way, you can bypass a large amount of the learning curve and step right into the art of practicing and refining your skill. The tips given to you in this chapter are ones that master marketers know and have been suggesting are going to be even more valuable going into 2021. By applying this information right away, you give yourself a jump start and help yourself have greater success going forward.

Keep Your Website Up to Date

First things first, if you want to be successful in digital marketing, you need to keep your website up to date. Your website is the page where people will end up going to either learn more about you, consume content by you, or even purchase from your business depending on how you have set your business up. If you want to have success in digital marketing, you need to make sure that you are keeping your website up to date, as this will provide a myriad of benefits for you and your online business.

The first benefit that you are going to gain from keeping your website up to date is that it will keep your page updated for SEO. This way, when people look for businesses like yours, they will be more likely to come across yours in the searches. SEO can be kept up to date on your website by updating information as needed, as well as by running a blog on your website. Even a basic blog with weekly or monthly updates can do wonders in keeping your website up to date, helping you to get located on SEO better.

The second major benefit that you gain from keeping your website up to date is the benefit of your customers being able to have updated information. This way, they are not coming to your website and finding outdated information, which can lead to many issues. This could cause your customers to try and get you to hold up an outdated sale, or it could cause them to believe that your business is no longer operating because the information is outdated. Keeping information up to date ensures that what they are receiving is relevant and recent.

Design and Evolve Your Customer Experience

Every single business, no matter how basic or intricate, needs a customer experience. Your customer experience accounts for the experience that your customers have when they interact with anything that has to do with your business. This includes marketing materials, the sales process, and the experience of getting anything from your business, such as products or services.

The more that you focus on your customer experience, the more you are going to be able to design an experience that is enjoyable and memorable for your audience. This way, when they think about your business, they do not just think about the great products that they gained from your business, but they also think about the great *experience* that they had. Furthermore, the experience can cause them to feel like they are a part of something special, which can actually increase their customer loyalty.

Whenever you are creating something for your business, think about how it is going to contribute to your customer experience. Think about how it will be for your customer to come across that piece of marketing material and to discover more about your business, and try to make this experience as enjoyable and easy as possible. Make it so that when your customer goes through this experience, it is personal, makes sense, and is easy for your customers to move forward with. This way, you can feel confident that you are cultivating an experience that is worth enjoying.

Get Your Business on Google

One step that many new businesses overlook, especially in 2020 and 2021, is getting your business on Google. Google is a search engine that has an archive of virtually every website and the company that is online, and if you want to be relevant online, you need to have your business on Google, too.

This goes for more than just having a website that Google retrieves. You also need to have a business that Google retrieves, especially if your business has a physical address.

You can get your business on Google by creating a Google business account and then uploading information about your business into it. Once you have, you will be prompted to verify some information about your business, allowing you to confirm with Google that it is, in fact, your business. After your business has been verified, Google will be able to showcase it to other people who are looking to find a business just like yours.

Master Your Call to Action

Back in the day, businesses were told to master their "elevator pitch," which would help people propose their business and encourage people to buy from them. These days, you need to master your call to action in your business in order to succeed, as this helps you become clear and confident in pitching your call to action. You can master your call to action by picking the one thing that you want people to do with your business, such as purchasing or ordering through you and then master pitching that calls to action. This means that you master the art of asking for the sale in posts, advertisements, and videos that you share online. You can do this by identifying how you want to create this call to action, and then by practicing it and using it as often as possible. Eventually, it will become easy and comfortable for you to share your call to action, helping other people feel more confident in you, too. This level of confidence and comfort will drastically increase your sales through your call to action because it will come across smooth and effortless, making it easier for people to trust in you and act on it.

Track Your Performance With Analytics

Finally, you need to track your performance with analytics. Many new business owners find this part to be particularly challenging because it can be hard to know what analytics you need to pay attention to and how you can use them to help you grow your business. When you are tracking your analytics, the primary thing you want to pay attention to is your level of engagement. If you have offered a link or a call to action, you also want to track the number of people who actually click the link or follow through on your call to action, too. These are the most basic analytics that will help you get started with tracking your performance in an easy manner.

Paying attention to these numbers is going to help you determine what you're best performing content is so that you can recreate more of that. You will also be able to determine which posts could be boosted or turned into paid marketing campaigns, helping you get even more content in front of your audience.

Chapter 11: Mistakes to Avoid

To help you even further advance your own knowledge and understanding of the subtleties of marketing, we can also explore mistakes that you need to avoid. In this chapter, we are going to cover five mistakes that you need to avoid when you are marketing your business to ensure that you do not make a fatal mistake from day one. Unfortunately, many marketers who are getting involved in digital marketing are known for coming across outdated or low-quality advice and putting it to work, only to find themselves completely destroying the reputation of themselves and their businesses. This can destroy your success far before you ever get a chance to begin, so you need to avoid these things if you are going to succeed with digital marketing.

Avoid Outdated Marketing Tactics

The first thing that you really need to avoid is outdated marketing tactics. Due to the nature of search engines, the advice shown to you is going to be the advice that is considered the most relevant to what you have gone in search of. This means that if you type in "digital marketing strategies that work," you might just find yourself coming across posts from the mid-to-late 2000s, which will be full of outdated advice. If you follow these strategies, you are going to find yourself marketing in the wrong era, which will result in you struggling to get in front of your audience and make a success with your business.

When you are looking for marketing strategies online, look to find ones that are still relevant. To do this, check the date of the post or article that you are reading to make sure that it was made within the last month or two. Never pay attention to anything created more than 6 months ago, as most of these strategies will have evolved in the past six months to become even more effective. Yes, marketing strategies evolve that quickly.

Avoid the "Abandoned Profile" Effect

One big mistake that people make with their businesses is creating a profile on a platform and then never updating it. Even if you do not intend on using a platform as a primary part of your strategy, you need to keep it up to date to avoid creating the "abandoned profile effect." If you create a profile and abandon it, even if you are active elsewhere online, you might lose possible customers. People who find you on that platform may think that you are no longer in business and not pursue you any further. Instead, you could upload that profile a couple of times per month with information to guide them back to your profiles where you are more active. This way, rather than missing out on the opportunity to connect with these individuals, you are funneling them over to one of your more active profiles.

Avoid Going into Digital Marketing Without a Plan

No matter how basic you think, your digital marketing business is if you go into it without a plan, you are going to find yourself struggling to make any form of success. In this book, we have given you tons of strategies and plans that you can use to make your business a success. The best way to take advantage of this information is to sit with it and make a specific plan for how you are going to put it to work in your business. This way, when it comes time for you to actually put it into action, you know what you are doing, and you can do it consistently. Remember, in digital marketing, consistency is key, and if you do not adhere to this rule, you are going to find yourself failing, fast.

Creating a plan is simple: you need to decide what your goal is and then choose a step-by-step approach for how you are going to reach that goal. For example, if your goal is to make passive income off of selling a course online, you could start by hosting the course as a live event and marketing it through social media and content marketing. Then, when it launches, you could sustain sales and your passive income using targeted paid advertising. Having your plan clearly defined means that you know what you need to be doing at all times, which will keep you moving toward total success in your business every single day. It will also prevent you from wasting time on activities that are not contributing to your bottom line.

Avoid Underestimating the Importance of All Devices

It is expected that by 2020, 4.78 *billion* people are going to own mobile devices. This means that close to 4.78 billion people are going to have access to the internet through their phones, making the mobile market a massive one. Even right now, we are already seeing many companies finding themselves struggling to stay afloat if they are not creating a presence that caters to both desktop and mobile. The simple truth is: people love using mobile devices and find them to be convenient and easy. If you are not optimized for mobile, people are going to look beyond you and to someone else instead, because it is not worth their time to try and fuss with your platform.

Trust that going into 2021; there are several competitors ready to take your place if you are not stepping up to the plate. When it comes to designing your online platforms, *always* think about both mobile and desktop. Make sure that your pictures are high enough quality and cropped right for both, make sure that your website is easy to navigate on both, and make sure that your buttons and links are all accessible on both. This way, more people have the capacity to do business with you, and you are more likely to earn more sales.

Avoid Not Diversifying Your Approach for Greater Reach

In the past, throwing something up and relying solely on PPC advertising was a great way to make an income online. People made hundreds of thousands of dollars doing this and had great success with it. In fact, these are the people who exposed just how easy making money online could be and are responsible for why so many people turned to the internet to try and make an income. That being said, these days, it does not pay to have such a simple approach to making money online.

This does not mean that you cannot still be just as passive in making your income, but it does mean that you need to make better use of a diversity of platforms and approaches if you are going to have success. If you still want your business to be highly passive, you simply need to take advantage of automated marketing or hire someone to manage your marketing for your passive income opportunity. Otherwise, you need to put effort into diversifying your approach and getting your business and marketing materials in front of as many people as possible. This is how you are going to not only create some success online but thrive online.

Chapter 12: The Power of Staying Relevant Through Conflict and Disaster

When chaos ensues, what are some actions a business can take to stay relevant? 2020 has shown us that when disaster strikes, the media can rapidly be taken over with a large focus on the current disaster, and nearly zero focus on anything else. This is not only relevant to 2020, though. Many businesses have faced the question of how to stay relevant when chaos ensues, whether it be because of a disaster going on in their industry, or a disaster going on in their geographical region. For example, a realtor selling houses amid a housing crisis may be worried about staying relevant and getting their job done, while a business that managed to survive in the wake of a tornado may be wondering if it is ethical to keep doing business.

The reality is, even when disaster strikes, regardless of what that disaster looks like, there needs to be a plan in place to help you stay relevant and continue doing business through that disaster. A failure to maintain your business and keep yourself relevant can lead to you being forced to shut your doors, which is not helpful to anyone. With that being said, staying relevant during normal times and staying relevant during peculiar times are two entirely different scenarios. Since we will not always be living among peculiar times, I want to enrich your business by offering you guidance on how to stay relevant during both sets of circumstances.

Staying Relevant During Regular Times Vs. Peculiar Times

Staying relevant during regular times and staying relevant during peculiar times are two different scenarios based on a little thing called ethics. When it comes to the individuals behind businesses, it may feel overwhelming to keep your brand relevant during peculiar times, because it may seem inappropriate to do "business as usual" when your community is suffering. That's because, in a way, it is inappropriate. However, there are shifts you can make to make your effort to stay relevant entirely appropriate. One starts with realizing that without your business, you are not making any money. Businesses cannot shut down or stop existing just because there is something major going on at that moment. In fact, businesses *must* keep running because they keep money flowing through the economy, and that money keeps the people being affected by disaster afloat during peculiar times.

If you are attempting to stay relevant during regular times, your primary focus is on keeping your brand fresh and updated so that you continue to be liked by your audience. All of the standard practices of leveraging trends, developing a sense of community within your audience, engaging with your community, and keeping up with the changing times are perfect when it comes to staying relevant during regular times. Your largest focus is to continue offering the latest and greatest so that when people are looking for an excellent experience, especially one that is specific to your niche, they look for that experience with you rather than with anyone else.

During peculiar times, that shifts. While you still need to keep up with all of the aforementioned elements of staying relevant, you also need to find a way to acknowledge and accommodate for the disaster that has struck your community. Whether that is your industry, your local community, or the global community, you need to know how to address it in a way that clearly acknowledges what is going on, positions you in a spot where you can help your audience, and makes it clear that you have compassion and empathy for what everyone is going through. Your audience wants to see the faces behind your brand that proves that you are right there with them, enduring the disaster together.

Deepening your sense of community, standing beside your audience, and becoming engaged with the people you are serving through your business is a powerful way to position yourself during a disaster. Firstly, it helps you stay relevant in a way that has compassion and consideration for the people who have been loyal to your brand in the past. Secondly, it allows you to play an integral role in helping your audience through that challenge. What ends up happening is they realize that you supported them when they needed it most, so they experience gratitude toward your brand, and they want to support you, too.

Sales, promotions, and other big events are still relevant and important, if not more important, during challenging times. Sales and promotions make it easier for your audience to get their hands on what you are selling, while celebrations or large events give them something positive to look forward to and enjoy. The key is to manage expectations and perceptions by marketing appropriately. For example, if you are doing a big launch and a disaster strikes, the solution is not necessarily to postpone the launch. It is also not to ignore the disaster and carry on with the launch as if to say you "do not care." Instead, it is to acknowledge the disaster and make it clear that you will carry on with the launch anyway to give your loyal followers something fun and exciting to look forward to after all of the tragedy they have faced recently. You might even plan something extra special to coincide with the event to take even better care of your audience throughout the process, such as a charitable donation, a giveaway or additional promotion, or something else to help give back to your customers.

When you are able to acknowledge and work mindfully around disasters, business can carry on as usual, and all of your standard practices for staying relevant continue to be true. The entire success of your ability to stay relevant starts and ends with your capacity to acknowledge disaster, express compassion for your audience, solidify your unity with your community, and give back in some way that genuinely supports your customers. If you manage these four steps effectively, you can carry on with "business as usual" despite anything going on in the world, which means you can confidently maintain and grow your business, even through tragedies.

Leveraging Trends to Stay Relevant

No matter what is going on in the world, one of the most powerful things you can do is leverage trends to stay relevant. Active trends show you what people care about, and allow you to directly serve people by engaging in what they are focused on. They provide an excellent opportunity for you to recognize where people's attention is going and allow you to use that attention to find ways to effectively remain at the center of people's attention.

The difference between trends during regular times, as opposed to during peculiar times, often lies within what types of things people are focusing on. During regular times, when the average population is relaxed and going about life as normal, trends are often fun and lighthearted. These trends are easy to get on board with because, as a brand, you can have fun and be lighthearted alongside your audience. You gain the opportunity to enjoy easygoing connection, effortless interactions, and your only focus is on how to incorporate these into your business in a more fun and enjoyable manner.

When disaster strikes, trends change. Often, people start focusing on heavier topics and things that may feel more challenging for you to address, especially from the perspective of your brand. The key is to acknowledge these trends and partake in both lighthearted and negative trends in a tasteful way. This shows your audience that you stand by them and that you care about what they care about, while also working toward bringing something fun and lighthearted in the mix for them to care about.

It is vitally important that, especially when particularly sensitive trends arise, you are considerate, compassionate, and direct in your approach. You should never attempt to avoid a topic that your audience cares about just because it is a sensitive topic because, in doing so, you show a disconnect between your passion and theirs. Brands who entirely ignore important topics are often seen as being superficial and insensitive, and may rapidly lose members of their audience, which can be devastating, especially if you have a small or medium-sized business. Essentially, you become irrelevant because you show your audience that you do not stand with them on *all* issues, only the ones that serve your growth.

While addressing something your audience cares about, especially when it is a heavy or sensitive topic, you must be extremely careful in your approach. Before you say anything, you must think about how your brand serves your audience and how your audience has come to expect being supported by your brand. You also need to consider what position you can take that will allow you to support your audience in a realistic manner, while still keeping your brand afloat. Then, you need to consider how you are going to convey this position through your messaging and wording and ensure that whatever you say is said in a way that remains compassionate and sensitive to the subject and everyone affected by it. It is a good idea to get someone else to read through your copy to ensure that you are marketing your brand in a way that truly emanates sensitivity and compassion.

Lastly, *never* try to connect your brand's campaign of addressing an important issue to a sale, promotion, or other offerings. Attempting to use a sensitive issue to sell more of your own products will come across as self-serving, insensitive, and will rapidly make your business irrelevant. You must make this a marketing campaign that is focused exclusively on your audience and benefit them, not your brand. In the long run, this will have a far greater impact on your bottom line than attempting to leverage a disaster to make more sales in your business.

Avoiding Tacky or Insensitive Campaigns

This should go without saying, but as you run any digital marketing campaigns, it is imperative that you avoid using tacky or insensitive campaigns. During the rise of 2020's disasters, some brands made the terrible choice of attempting to leverage this tragic trend as an opportunity to earn more sales in their businesses. It may seem like a no-brainer not to do this, but unfortunately, it happened. A good example of a campaign that failed included a sandwich company offering free facemasks to any customer that purchased two sandwiches. While something like this may not seem obviously insensitive, at the time, it was challenging for professionals to acquire masks, which meant this company was hoarding them and using them as a way to increase their sales during a pandemic. Tacky.

During any trend, regardless of whether there is a tragedy going on or not, you should always take time to audit how your marketing campaigns will look and sound to your audience. They may seem brilliant to you, but you need to ensure that they are going to be received in an intended way by your audience first. If there is a chance your audience will not get what you meant or may take it the wrong way, you need to adjust your campaign, so there is no room for accidental misinterpretation.

Another thing you need to be aware of is the importance of running service-based campaigns. In fact, one way that the aforementioned sandwich company could have increased their sales, without looking tacky, through a service-based campaign would have been to offer free masks to anyone who dropped in, regardless of purchase. Or, they could have donated all of their excess masks to the local health unit and run a campaign that said something like, "Thanks to your loyalty, we were able to donate 15,000 masks to local hospitals!" These campaigns would have been entirely focused on them giving back and would have developed a positive association around their brand in a way that recognized the current trends in a compassionate and sensitive manner. As a result, they likely would have seen a major influx in sales due to the fact that people would have wanted to offer them greater support so that they could do even more to give back.

Always be extremely mindful of what your campaigns look like, and always adjust them if you are ever doubtful about how your audience will receive a campaign. While being edgy and pushing boundaries can be a great marketing strategy, being insensitive is not.

Deepening the Sense of Community Within Your Brand

If you want to make a power move in your ability to gain and maintain relevancy within your brand, you need to deepen the sense of community within your brand's audience. Brands who are not tapping into the power of the community are doing themselves a disservice by creating a situation where they have to repeatedly gain the attention, trust, and respect of their audience over and over again. If you manage to remain relevant enough to continue earning sales, you will be sinking insane amounts of money, time, and effort into getting those sales because as soon as you earn sales, you will lose the attention and interest of your audience. Then, you will be back at ground zero, and you will have to do it all over again.

Building a sense of community around your brand means that your brand becomes an entity that people care about. Now, rather than coming, buying, and disappearing until you lure them back with great marketing, you are encouraging them to join you and stay with you, whether you have active sales going on or not. In a sense, you leverage the parasocial relationship or the one-sided relationship your audience shares with your brand, to create a sort of lasting friendship. This keeps your audience investing more emotional energy and time into your brand because now they feel a sense of connection, and they want to keep your brand in their circuit.

There are two adjustments you can make to the digital marketing strategy that will allow you to deepen your sense of community and grow your brand to greater heights. The first is in your targeted campaigns, and the second is in the way that you engage with your community.

In your targeted campaigns, always make an effort to clarify how everything is about community. Are you selling a new pair of sneakers? Great, which friends should your audience show those sneakers to first? Or, should they take a special photograph of their sneakers and upload it with your community hashtag, so they feel like a part of your community? Do this with any product or service you might be selling. Always look for a way to get your audience to share it with their community, with your community, or both, as this increases the idea of community being an integral part of your brand. The result? They feel more connected to you, and they stay more loyal to you.

In your everyday engagement, create personal posts that resemble something someone would share on their personal page. Ask questions, share pictures of your brand's team, or of something going on behind the scenes with your company, share funny pictures your audience might enjoy, and otherwise share content you believe they would like. Creating a brand page that resembles a personal timeline means that your brand's entity is being personified, making it even easier for people to relate to it. The outcome is that your audience will develop a sense of loyalty and will personally seek you out and invest in your brand, the same way you are investing in your community.

Engaging In the Way Your Audience Is Engaging

One of your primary digital marketing research tasks should be to spend time observing your audience so that you can better understand how they engage with each other, with brands, and with your brand, specifically. Observing your audience allows you to more clearly understand what their behaviors are like, what their preferences are, what dislikes they have, and other important pieces of information about them. The more you understand what your audience likes and dislikes, and what their natural engagement sounds like, the easier it is for you to identify opportunities to engage with your audience in a way that they will understand.

Your goal as a brand is to talk the same talk and walk the same walk as your audience. You want them to feel a sense of connection with your brand by being able to relate with it, understand it, and feel as though they can develop a personal connection with it. This is how you get into their "inner circle." It is easy to understand this by taking a quick look at basic human psychology. Think about yourself for a moment. Chances are, there are people you absolutely don't like, people you don't know, people you don't mind, people you like, and people you love. The people you love are the only ones you invest consistent, significant energy into, while the people you like may get some of that energy, too. Everyone else is either ignored or receives negative attention from you.

Likewise, other people have this same circle around them. They, too, will invest the majority of their energy into the people they love, and then they will invest a small amount of energy into the people they like.

You want to turn your brand into an entity that they can personally relate with, and get it into the inner circle of being an entity they love. If you are in the circle of "don't mind" or beyond, you will either receive no attention or negative attention from these individuals. If you are in the circle of "like," you may seem some attention, but you will have to push hard to continue to receive that attention, and it may be inconsistent at best. But if you are in the circle of "love," your brand will receive attention from your audience in a way that completely transforms the face of your company, while also maximizing your sales potential.

How do you get to be in the "love" circle? You share mutual interests, concerns, passions, mannerisms, behaviors, vocabularies, and other key aspects of a personality makeup. Even though your brand may not be based around a single person, you can create an entity for your brand that can easily be personified by your audience through developing these human-like characteristics as a part of your brand identity and profile. As a result, you find yourself relating with your audience far more effectively, and receiving far more love and attention from your audience, which leads to significantly greater sales, too.

Keeping Up With the Changing Times

Lastly, you need to keep up with the changing times. Part of staying relevant is advancing into new technology and leveraging new tools as they become available to you. Whether it is new techniques you can use to improve your customer service, new software you can use to improve your online user experience, or new tools you can use to improve different aspects of your business processes, you need to keep up with the changing times.

Companies that allow themselves to grow outdated become irrelevant in the eyes of customers because they are using technology and techniques that actually reduce the customer experience. The purpose of evolution and advancement is improvement, which is why companies are always staying at the front of these improvements. They are always looking for ways to use these new and advanced technologies to boost their improvement and increase their ability to provide a better customer experience.

Certain companies, specifically those which intend to have a traditional feel to them, may be reluctant to add new technology for fear of losing their ability to offer a traditional experience. In these cases, the best opportunity is to use improved technology but implement it in a manner that provides an exceptional traditional-like experience. As well, remember that the traditional "energy" of a brand is often created through the interactions of customers and customer service representatives, so you can easily maximize that energy through effective customer service training that maximizes traditional service.

Anytime you implement a new technology or technique into your business, regardless of whether you have a traditional brand or not, you should always look at how that resource fits into your overall brand and how it can be best used to improve customer experience. While you do need to keep up with evolution, you should not rush the advancements as this can lead to detrimental side effects, which ultimately destroy the customer experience and could put a serious damper on your brand's reputation. Instead of rushing the process, think it through, consider how a resource could be best used, and phase it in with careful consideration and monitoring.

Then, use it as a clear marketing point. Anytime you create an advancement that directly benefits the consumer, which all advancements should, you want to talk about it and let your audience know. This shows them that you are constantly doing everything you can to improve their customer experience with your brand.

One last thing I must point out when it comes to keeping up with the times is digital marketing technology specifically. Technology advances and fast. You must always be paying attention to changes that are occurring in the advertising platforms you are already using, as well as watching for new platforms or marketing opportunities that become available. Constant, on-going research allows you to spot changes immediately and leverage them right away, which means you end up with far more effective campaigns.

You should be researching existing platforms, campaign rules on different platforms, algorithms, marketing trends, organic and paid marketing strategies, and new platforms that may be emerging. You should also be researching your target audience so you can pay close attention to what their preferences are and how they might shift over time so you can accommodate for that in your marketing strategies. The more receptive and responsive you are with your campaigns, the more success you will have with them.

Chapter 13: The Latest Trends in Digital Marketing

You will hear it constantly: digital marketing is always changing, and if you want to be successful with it, you must be prepared to ride the waves of change. What worked two years ago, one year ago, or even six months ago, will no longer be the most effective marketing strategy. These days, you must be paying attention to the day to day shifts if you will be successful in keeping your brand ahead of the competition and driving your way to the top.

At the beginning of 2020, it was predicted that platforms other than Facebook would emerge as being stronger and more useful to digital marketers, and that has remained mostly true. It was also predicted that new platforms would rise, automation would takeover, and yet personalization and individual attention would maintain importance and be required if a brand were going to be successful with their marketing campaigns and strategies. So far, all of these predictions have come true.

As we are now halfway into 2020, I wanted to update this book with plenty of excellent content that would help you understand how these predictions are coming true, and how you can use them to help you launch your business into even greater levels of success. We will address each of these claims, discuss what they mean, and understand how you can implement these changes to your digital marketing approach. In doing so, your brand will be far more likely to stay relevant while also being able to leverage that relevancy in a way that increases your sales potential.

Facebook Is Losing Grounds with the Younger Demographic

People have been predicting Facebook's decline for a few years now, and while this may not be the case yet, we are definitely starting to see Facebook reach its peak. These days, 41% of Facebook users are over the age of 65, which is a highly niche audience that is not exactly popular to target among online business owners. When marketers start to see terms like "losing grounds" or "decline," it can be easy to automatically assume that a certain marketing strategy is becoming irrelevant. However, that is not necessarily the case. In some situations, it may be a good idea to hop off board. When it comes to an icon like Facebook, though, it is often a better idea to take it slow and play your cards right.

Despite the fact that Facebook is losing grounds with the younger demographic, there are still 51% of users who are under the age of 65, and a good chunk of those are going t be a part of your target audience. This means that Facebook needs to be a part of your marketing strategy. However, the way it fits into your marketing strategy should not be the same as it would have been in years gone by. Disregard marketing strategies that suggest Facebook should be your primary platform, because this is unlikely to be a sustainable platform long term, and it could result in you minimizing your growth potential or setting yourself up for trouble in the future.

As a part of your strategy, you *should* have a Facebook page. You should also post on it and drive traffic there, as this turns it into an active spot that will effectively attract more audience members your way. What should change is not whether or not you use Facebook, but what you do with the traffic you gain on Facebook. In 2020 and beyond, you should be driving that traffic to another platform, like Instagram, where you can post in a way that is more interactive for younger demographics. Through that, you will find the ability to connect and engage with your audience better, and they will be more likely to convert better.

One other reason why you should not leave Facebook behind is because Facebook is a necessary component of Instagram advertising. You must have a Facebook business page linked to your Instagram page if you are going to do any paid advertising since all paid advertisements are run through Facebook's ad center.

Instagram Is the Most Popular Platform for Younger Kids

Instagram is an incredibly popular platform, and it is actually gaining traction around the youngest demographics, too, such as children and teenagers. Because of the visual content and the ability to see new products and games that people are playing, younger crowds love being a part of this platform. That breaks down to two things for your advertising strategy.

Firstly, if you are targeting any generation under 65 years old, you need to be on Instagram. If you are targeting even younger generations, like those under the age of 25, Instagram will likely be one of the most successful platforms for you to use. Here, you will find that exact audience, and you will be able to create content that caters to their preferences for content consumption, too.

The second thing you need to consider is subject matter and targeting. Because so many younger children are on Instagram, it is important that you are especially careful about the types of content you are posting. If you are specifically targeting young adults over the age of 20, you can get away with more swearing and edgy content. If, however, you are targeting anyone who is in any way a part of a family unit with younger children, such as parents or the younger children themselves, you must keep your content PG. This means no swearing, adequate coverage on models, and portraying content that is acceptable for younger children. Another important thing to consider is what messages you are sending, as parents will be unlikely to let their children or teenagers follow you if you are sending messages that are likely to make them feel inadequate or develop unhealthy world views. Always be considerate of your audience, and of other people who may accidentally find their way into your audience.

Properly Designed Chatbots Are Excellent for Customer Service

Chatbots are becoming more widely acceptable, and many businesses, no matter what their size may be, are starting to rely on them as a business strategy. These days, people's attention spans are incredibly short, and most people have very little desire to sit around and wait for a response. If you are a smaller business, prompt replies may be challenging, especially as you start gaining traction and receiving more inquiries from your customers. Chatbots can help.

It is important that if you use chatbots, you are upfront about it, and that you do not attempt to hide the fact that you are using an automated service. Some brands even name their chatbots so that when their customers message in, they know they are receiving a message from an automated bot, but the message feels more personal because the bot has a name and speaks in a conversational tone. You can program yours as you see fit.

The benefit of chatbots comes in two fold. First, your chatbot improves your response time, lets your customers know you have received their inquiries, and creates a sense of instant gratification for anyone that is looking to get a response from your business. Second, chatbots can be programmed to answer basic questions or provide basic support to people. On Facebook, for example, you can program common questions and answers into your chatbot so that when people message your page, they can receive answers to some common questions they may have. You can use these questions to answer anything from shipping-related questions to how your customers can get prompt service or anything else that seems relevant to your business model. Make sure the questions are actually commonly asked questions; however, as this ensures the bot will truly be helpful to your customers.

It is also vital to ensure that someone is monitoring the inbox so that prompt replies can be given even after the chatbot has done its part. Even though they have received some form of communication, customers will still not want to be kept waiting on responses.

Messaging Apps Are Excellent Tools for Marketing Through

Chatbots are excellent when it comes to customer service, but they are not the only way you can spruce up your marketing strategy. So far, in 2020, we see messaging apps as being excellent marketing tools that can be used to inform audiences of new promotions or offers, as well as upcoming launches or events that a business may be having.

Most messaging apps work by having people automatically subscribed anytime they message your business page for any reason. They can easily opt out by unchecking the box in the top right corner of their messenger app, which will allow them to stop receiving automated messages from you.

For those who want to receive messages from you, though, this is a unique way of sending them. Messaging apps provide the opportunity for it to make it feel like you are directly addressing your audience and sending them a private, personal update about what is going on in your business. Because the messaging approach already has a personalized feel, it is important that you capitalize on that by writing messages in a way that sounds personalized, too. By combining automation with personalization, you will be capitalizing on the two major trends moving into 2021, before 2021 even hits.

Video Content Must Be Used for Your Brand to Stay Relevant

As of 2020, video content is no longer strongly recommended or recognized as a trending content style. It is now recognized as *the* content style to be creating, and if you are not creating video for your brand, you are seriously hurting your growth. Studies have shown that failure to produce video not only stunts your growth but can actually have people ditching your page in favor of people in the same industry who are producing video content.

What type of video content you create depends on what industry you are in, what you are marketing, and where you are posting that content. On advertisements to new audience members, for example, your videos are likely to be short and based on building awareness around who you are and what you have to offer. With advertisements to existing audience members, however, you may create video content that is designed to teach people how to use the products they have already purchased, or how to get the most out of your services.

Educational- and entertainment-based video content are currently the two categories to be in right now. If you can combine them, that's even better. Educational-based video content includes any content that educates your audience on your industry or something specific within your industry, your brand, or something specific within your brand, or anything similar. Entertainment-based video content should be focused on entertaining people in a way that is relevant to your industry, such as making jokes your industry's audience would understand, or purposefully using products wrong or in weird or unusual ways. Try to be as creative as you possibly can, and shoot in the highest quality you can (most smart phones shook in 4K now) while also doing some basic edits to improve your content quality. This way, you are more likely to get traction with your videos, since they will be posted alongside so many other videos that are also competing for the attention of your audience.

Context In Your Content Matters As Much As Quality Does

As our social climate changes, the way you word things matters. Online, and through most advertising mediums, there is very little room for you to give context to what you are saying or what you are creating. This means that people can easily misinterpret what you mean, which can result in your brand taking a serious hit to its reputation as well as its sales. If you are a smaller brand, this hit could be devastating.

To give you an example of how sensitive this issue may be, I want to turn your attention to a national insurance company that launched a campaign at the start of the 2020 pandemic. Their campaign encouraged people to high five over great insurance rates. The campaign was planned well in advance of the pandemic, and the high five was intended to promote a community-based feel by encouraging connection with people you care about. Unfortunately, it launched around the same time global shut downs began, which resulted in the context being entirely wrong to the current global climate at the time of its launch. The result? The brand took major backlash from many people across social media platforms.

It is important to understand that most audiences are entirely unaware of the work that goes into creating campaigns, or the amount of time it takes to get one out. Further, they are not necessarily going to interpret those campaigns accurately, and that can lead to unfortunate circumstances. Always pause, review your campaign, and look at it from as many different angles as possible. Better yet, have a group of go-to people who can review your campaigns for you to ensure there is nothing possibly harmful or negative hidden within your campaign. This way, when you launch a campaign, you know for absolute certain that you will not accidentally send the wrong message or hurt anyone in your audience due to a lack of awareness or a misinterpretation of the context of your message.

Email Marketing Campaigns Should Be More Personalized

Email marketing campaigns are still popular, despite the number of people who have suggested that email marketing has "died" over the past few years. Emails are still an important aspect of business because when you own an email list, *you* own that email list. No social media algorithm or online giant can take that list away from you or somehow destroy your ability to connect with your audience. For that reason, you should still be capturing emails and creating content for your email audience so that, in the event, something does go wrong, you still have direct access to them in a way that they are used to receiving content through.

With your email marketing campaigns, it is important that you personalize them. These days, marketing campaigns can be personalized by breaking your email list into segments and creating content for each individual segment. Most major email marketing platforms will help you create these segments, and they can be created based on the geographical location of your audience members, their unique demographics, or their activity within your emails. For example, if someone clicks on one of your links in your emails, they can be seen as someone who is more likely to engage. Therefore you can specifically send them content they can engage with. If you have people who do not click links, though, you may lighten the number of links in the email and instead offer value right there in that email to encourage them to start paying closer attention.

As you break your list up into segments, ensure that you leverage those segments in the most powerful ways possible. Write content that is highly specific to that segment, as it will feel like you are writing content for each individual member of your audience. Again, automation and personalization are two major trends that will explode in 2021, so this is an important topic to pay attention to and start mastering right away.

Interactive Content Is the Mainstream Marketing Strategy of Choice

As parasocial relationships grow and the dynamics shift, audiences in a parasocial relationship want to be acknowledged and invited to communicate with the brand or media persona of the parasocial relationship. This means that interactive content is becoming the mainstream marketing strategy of choice, and the popularity it gains continues to grow.

Interactive content means that you are cultivating content that encourages people to engage with you. Rather than being recognized or paused over while someone aimlessly scrolls, you are using call to action's (CTA's) as an opportunity to invite people to interact with your brand. This requires a three step process: you create content that encourages engagement, people engage, and you engage back. It is vital that you engage back, as this shows that you are looking at genuinely engaging with your audience, and you are not just asking for engagement to boost your algorithm. While all people may not realize that the purpose of this is often a play for the algorithm, they will realize that you are asking for them to engage but that you are not returning that energy. The lack of a two-way connection will result in them essentially ignoring your CTA because you train them that they will gain nothing from engaging.

Interactive content can be created by asking questions, starting polls, encouraging people to share specific content using your hashtag, inviting people to create videos of them using your products or services, or even asking them to leave some sort of response on your content. It is important that your request for interaction is interesting and that it leads to meaningful engagement in both directions, as this is how you can ensure your audience will respond.

When it comes time to return that engagement, be sure to respond to as many comments as you can. If people use your brand hashtag, like their posts and thank them for using your hashtag. When followers share something that features your brand, reshare their post so that you can feature them in front of your audience, and thank them for sharing content. These types of interactive posts are excellent as they really build that feeling of friendship between you and your audience, which results in them experiencing a much higher sense of loyalty to you and your brand. That loyalty will always convert into financial gains, as long as you respect the loyalty and continue to build it by also remaining loyal to your audience.

Chapter 14: The 2021 Digital Marketing Forecast

If you want to get ahead by leaps and bounds, you need to not only know what is going on in 2020, but also be aware of what trends are likely to emerge and develop in 2021. The sooner you begin researching these trends, the more you will understand them, and the sooner you will be able to get on board in a way that generates powerful results. This means you will be far more likely to capitalize on these trends and maximize your growth, well ahead of everyone else.

In the digital marketing world, audiences both want and need to see their favorite brands engaging in the latest trends before anyone else. If you wait too long, your audience has already seen it happen in other brands, and they are not particularly interested in paying attention once you do it, because it is no longer fresh and exciting. In the meantime, they may even find themselves drawn into other brands that are your direct competition because those other brands got to the trends before you did.

While we can never guarantee exactly what trends will arise in any given year, we can predict based on predictive measuring models and research collected by people who are experts in the marketing fields. What these experts have discovered is as follows.

Automation Meets Personalization, and the Balance Matters

Technology is aggressively advancing, and with it, more things are becoming automated every single year. In the past, businesses shied away from automation for fear of losing that intimate connection with their audience. Since most audiences were new to the idea and were unaware of how automation worked, or how it affected their interactions with a company, many also shied away from interacting with businesses that were heavily automated.

These days, automation is far more accepted among virtually every audience and is exploding in popularity. The simple fact is, automation provides much faster service, creates much more seamless experiences for audiences, and ensures that brands are able to capitalize on the short attention span of the average human in the modern era.

In order to successfully grow your business, you need to integrate automation strategies into your business and load those automation strategies with personalization. The key to achieving this is through how you write your content and how you target your content. Content should always be written in a way that unifies your brand with your audience, ideally on an individual level. You can also target your audience through segments, allowing you to create content that is very specific to the individual segments of your audience. For example, if you sell wellness products to women, you might segment them by age and level of fitness, then create content that caters to each age and fitness category. This allows you to heavily personalize content, while also integrating automation strategies.

Non-Linear Advertising Captures Attention

Non-linear advertising refers to advertising that does not follow any structured experience. These days, people click on what looks interesting, and they come across brands and information in all sorts of places. Previously, leading your audience through a linear purchasing experience was a great way to keep them focused and encourage them to purchase your products. These days, their attention span is way too short for that.

Rather than trying to draw your audience through a linear purchasing experience, you want to create several micro-exposure and micro-purchasing experiences that suit the non-linear behavior of most audiences these days.

Micro-exposure experiences should be focused on creating exposure to your brand or products within about 1 minute or less. These posts or campaigns should *always* point toward a micro-purchasing experience in case someone wants to learn more. Micro-purchasing experiences should be short, to the point, and easy for your audience to purchase through.

They are not going to purchase, though. Not right away, at least. Studies show that a consumer must see something at least 13 times before they decide whether or not they are truly interested in it, and up to another 13-14 times more before they actually purchase it. This leads to them seeing it around 26-27 times before they go ahead and hit "buy." Your micro-experiences, then, are focused on successfully achieving as many of those exposures as possible, all with positive associations, so your audience is more likely to purchase through you.

Keep in mind that while micro-experiences are important, you should still have at least one significant experience, or location online, where your audience can get *all* of the information. This way, when they are ready to purchase, they have access to all of the information and answers they would need in order to hit "buy." In a sense, this is automation as it automates the educational and question and answering part of the purchasing experience. Keep in mind, though; there should only be one key area where this large selling experience happens. All other exposures should be short, sweet, and to-the-point.

Marketing Automation Is a Powerhouse, and It Must Be Used Correctly

Marketing automation is a powerhouse, as it has been for at least a few years now. Previously, automation was used to drive people through lengthy sales processes that escalated them from small end purchases to large ticket items. The idea was to condition the mind of your buyer, so they would be more likely to purchase, while also proving your value at every step of the process. For example, you would sell them a $15 product and prove that it was well worth the value, which would make them more likely to purchase the $50 product you were going to sell them next. While they were being conditioned to buy, you were making money off of them.

This approach still works, but it needs to be done in an important way. The days of single-page websites with a wall of text and videos are gone. People do not have the attention span or the care to be drawn through such a lengthy experience. Instead, you need to automate your marketing so that it provides several automated micro-experiences over a period of time, as this is how you will build connections and rapport with your audience.

Automated social media posts, emails, blog posts, and even entire automated launch sequences are all powerful when it comes to digital marketing. You should also be leveraging paid advertising, which allows you to get in front of your audience without having to put in all the effort of organic marketing. While organic marketing can still get you a great deal of growth, and can explode your engagement, it can also be much slower. These days, a combined approach that is developed through smart automation is the best way to grow your audience and generate successful conversions, too.

Voice Search Marketing Is an Essential

Voice search usage is growing, especially with the introduction of digital assistants like Google Home and Amazon Alexa. Believe it or not, voice search marketing is a relevant marketing strategy, and it is becoming an essential one at that. Voice search marketing is accomplished by developing a website that directly answers questions that people are most likely to have, and that offers clear easy-to-read answers. The benefit here is that digital assistants can easily scan your website for relevant answers and read off of your website to the person who has asked such a question.

In order to get found by digital assistants, you need to use white hat SEO to optimize your page and increase your chances of being discovered. The higher you can rank with SEO, the more likely you will be to get found on voice searches. It is important that you focus on all SEO strategies, including maximizing your viewership, using proper keywords and in a proper ratio, and otherwise providing high-quality content, so your page is more likable. Increasing the social recognition behind your brand name is another great way to increase your rank and get found by voice searches, as well, as digital assistants are more likely to look for reputable sources, and they define a reputable source based on web popularity and quality of traffic.

Content Marketing Should Be Content Selling

Content marketing and content selling are now one and the same. In the past, content marketing was about gaining attention from your audience and getting your business out there. Content selling was about using that attention and credibility you gained from marketing and turning it into sales. The time is coming where both can be done at the same time.

Previously, in all industries, sales were achieved by directly advertising a product and offering the sale. These days, selling can be achieved by marketing a product and then offering a spot for someone to further explore that product on their own accord. This means that you are focused solely on creating marketing-based content, but you are always offering interested parties the opportunity to go to sales-based content if they prefer. This means that the 80/20 approach is fading and that your consumers no longer have to wait for that 20% content to arise before purchasing from you.

To successfully create the merge in your own business, be sure to have high-quality evergreen content, likely on your website, that can be used to conduct the sale. Everything else, especially on social media, should be solely based on attraction marketing strategies, and then should include the option for people to "learn more" at that link. This way, you are always marketing *and* selling, while leveraging the best attraction marketing strategies from all angles.

Hyper-Targeted Advertising

Hyper-targeted advertising is one of the best quality strategies you can use when it comes to combining automation and personalization. Hyper-targeted advertising is the same as segmenting your audience, as it allows you to focus specific pieces of content to the part of your audience that is most likely to enjoy it. This means that brands need to be focused on making content that will serve each character profile within their audience, assuming that there are many who make up your entire audience.

It may seem stressful or even irresponsible to make such niched down content, but the reality is that it is far more likely to gain traction since it has the power of being far more personalized. For example, let's say your audience contains women who are aged 35-65. You might create hyper-targeted content that is oriented for mothers for your younger demographic, while creating hyper-targeted content that is oriented for grandmothers or retirees for your older demographic. This way, you are able to actually personalize that content and make it sound like you are speaking directly to one individual, rather than to a group of individuals.

The benefit of hyper-targeted advertising, aside from maximizing personalization, is that it allows you to specify your paid campaigns to a hyper-targeted audience, too. These audiences are typically so niched that they cost far less to get in front of because it is unlikely that other campaigns are targeting for those exact placements. Of course, ensure your paid advertisements are also written in a way that emphasizes this hyper-targeted approach, as this will be far more likely to guarantee your success.

Maximizing Your Digital Marketing Budget Will Matter

As of 2020, companies who want to maintain their current position should spend 5% of their total revenue on marketing. Those who want to grow should spend 10% of their total revenue on marketing. The rest of that revenue goes into other business-related expenses.

In 2020 and 2021, you should be as close to that 10% margin as possible, if not aiming for as high as 15%. Especially for starter businesses, you need to get your company in front of as many eyes as possible, in as short of time as possible to secure excellent results.

Not only should you be spending as much as you can on marketing, but you also need to be spending that money wisely. After all, there is no point in increasing your marketing budget if you are not going to be seeing the same results from your campaigns. It is important to note that going into 2021, marketing on major platforms like Facebook and Google will change, as they are pushing for more whitehat marketing and less blackhat marketing. This means that they want you to use extremely honest, integrity-oriented marketing strategies that are considerate of their audience, and that genuinely help their audience feel good. This way, their audience is more likely to enjoy these campaigns and engage with them. At the end of the day, these platforms must focus on their audience, first, as their audience is responsible for making them big enough to be able to support their advertising programs in the first place.

It will be extremely important to read the latest marketing information on a weekly basis, at least, to know exactly what is going on with these platforms and their marketing rules, as this will keep you on track and generating massive success from your campaigns.

Streamlined Marketing Strategies Will Change The Game

Did you know the average company uses around 92 different platforms to run their marketing campaigns through? For smaller or startup businesses, the number is likely much lower, but it stands to prove that there are still many different platforms incorporated into the average business marketing strategy. This means that there are a lot of different areas that require your attention, as you need to make sure they are being optimized to deliver content on time without becoming a financial drain on your company.

Going into 2021, you need to streamline your marketing strategy as much as possible. It is no longer reasonable to have a small or startup business where you define an approach and then juggle several different platforms to make it happen. You need to have a defined order of operations and a clear system for managing your results if you are going to generate success with your business.

Starting from day one, focus on just one platform at a time and define an exact strategy for automating your marketing content, monitoring analytics, reviewing results, and then starting all over again. You should also always look for automation tools within these platforms, and educate yourself on how to leverage those automation tools for the best results. This way, you know that your approach is thorough and does not allow for anything, from campaigns to money, to slip through the cracks. If you find that any of the automation tools seem overwhelming or confusing, YouTube offers plenty of excellent videos that will show you exactly how you can use these tools in the most effective manner possible. Give yourself a few days to get used to using them before adding more automation to your plate, but make your end-goal to automize as much as possible to reinforce your streamlined approach.

It is important that you routinely double-check these orders of operations to ensure that they are continuing to serve your business. If you find at any time that your order of operations is allowing for anything to slip through the cracks, immediately change it and *write those defined changes down.*
Keeping all of this written down ensures that you are always on top of things and that your system is as streamlined as possible. In the end, this is better for your audience, and this is better for your business, too.

Conclusion

Digital marketing has been around for more than two decades now, and it continues to be an incredibly powerful resource for earning an income online. Whether you want to be completely hands-on, or totally passive in how you earn an income online, you need to know how to tap into digital marketing for success in your online business.

Now that you have read *Digital Marketing for Beginners 2021*, you have access to not only all of the best information about digital marketing but also the most relevant information about digital marketing. These steps are proven, as they have already generated massive success for businesses in 2020, and they are sure to help you generate massive success in 2021, too. By following these strategies, you can do everything in a way that is up to date with modern standards, and that is going to help you really get out there and make a name for yourself, and fast.

Remember: digital marketing is all about strategy, purpose, and clarity. You also need to make sure that you are staying ahead of the curve by staying up to date on new trends so that your marketing always reflects the latest in digital marketing strategies. If you fall behind or find yourself using out of date marketing strategies, you will find that your audience fails to keep up with you because they do not enjoy following your outdated practices.

Beyond using the strategies that we already know to be successful in 2020, it can be helpful to focus on what you can do to set yourself up for success in 2021 and beyond. The sooner you start researching these budding trends, the sooner you will be able to fully understand them and effectively execute them in your own marketing strategies. As always, those who are first on the scene to a new strategy will always be the most successful with it, assuming they use it correctly.

With all of this information in mind, it is time for you to get clear on your digital marketing strategy and move forward! If you have not already, you need to identify what your income channel is going to be so that you know exactly where you are going to be earning your income from online. Then, you need to identify the best possible strategy for getting your content out there so that people know you exist and have the opportunity to shop with you. You can build your strategy using some basic research on the industry that you have chosen, and then following the map in this book. Simply identify the most popular form of marketing for your chosen industry, and then follow the "Combine ____ marketing with other digital marketing strategies" guides at the end of each marketing chapter to discover what method is going to work best for you and your audience.

Lastly, if you enjoyed this book and felt that it supported you with creating a successful strategy for digital marketing going into 2020, we ask that you please take the time to review it on Amazon Kindle. Your feedback would be greatly appreciated!

Thank you, and best of luck!

CPSIA information can be obtained
at www.ICGtesting.com
Printed in the USA
LVHW090913210122
708838LV00027B/906